PREFACE

1. Scope

This publication provides doctrinal guidance for planning and executing barrier, obstacle, and mine warfare for joint operations as they relate to strategic, operational, and tactical mobility and countermobility across the range of military operations.

2. Purpose

This publication has been prepared under the direction of the Chairman of the Joint Chiefs of Staff. It sets forth joint doctrine to govern the activities and performance of the Armed Forces of the United States in operations and provides the doctrinal basis for interagency coordination and for US military involvement in multinational operations. It provides military guidance for the exercise of authority by combatant commanders and other joint force commanders (JFCs) and prescribes joint doctrine for operations, education, and training. It provides military guidance for use by the Armed Forces in preparing their appropriate plans. It is not the intent of this publication to restrict the authority of the JFC from organizing the force and executing the mission in a manner the JFC deems most appropriate to ensure unity of effort in the accomplishment of the overall objective.

3. Application

a. Joint doctrine established in this publication applies to the Joint Staff, commanders of combatant commands, subunified commands, joint task forces, subordinate components of these commands, and the Services.

b. The guidance in this publication is authoritative; as such, this doctrine will be followed except when, in the judgment of the commander, exceptional circumstances dictate otherwise. If conflicts arise between the contents of this publication and the contents of Service publications, this publication will take precedence unless the Chairman of the Joint Chiefs of Staff, normally in coordination with the other members of the Joint Chiefs of Staff, has provided more current and specific guidance. Commanders of forces operating as part of a multinational (alliance or coalition) military command should follow multinational doctrine and procedures ratified by the United States. For doctrine and procedures not ratified by the United States, commanders should evaluate and follow the multinational command's doctrine and procedures, where applicable and consistent with US law, regulations, and doctrine.

For the Chairman of the Joint Chiefs of Staff:

WILLIAM E. GORTNEY
VADM, USN
Director, Joint Staff

Intentionally Blank

SUMMARY OF CHANGES
REVISION OF JOINT PUBLICATION 3-15
DATED 26 APRIL 2007

- US Land Mine Policy changes incorporated fully into this publication. As of 1 January 2011, US forces are no longer authorized to utilize persistent land mines anywhere (previously allowed only in Korea through end of 2010).

- Changed acronym for mine warfare from MIW to MW.

- Revised Appendix A, "Reporting"

  — No longer need reports for intention to lay, initiation, and completion of conventional minefields.

  — Modified reports for reporting mines of any type laid by non-US forces.

  — Added report for unexploded ordnance/explosive remnants of war.

- Revised Appendix E, "Maritime Mine Warfare and Mine Countermeasures Organization and Capabilities."

- Deleted Appendix G, "Improvised Explosive Devices Defeat." All counter-improvised explosive device material now in Joint Publication 3-15.1, *Counter-Improvised Explosive Device Operations.*

- Revised Appendix H, "References."

- Changed antipersonnel mines to antipersonnel land mines.

- Changed antitank mines to anti-vehicular land mines.

Intentionally Blank

TABLE OF CONTENTS

EXECUTIVE SUMMARY
COMMANDER'S OVERVIEW

- **Presents the Framework and Context for Employing and Countering Obstacles**

- **Discusses Joint Planning Considerations**

- **Explains Barriers, Obstacles, and Land Mines Role in Land Operations**

- **Describes Mine Warfare in Maritime Operations**

Framework and Context for Employing and Countering Obstacles

In many types of operations, joint forces can employ obstacles as a significant force multiplier.

Joint forces should be prepared to encounter barriers, obstacles (including improvised explosive devices [IEDs], mines, and other unexploded explosive ordnance [UXO]) and to conduct mine warfare (MW), employing mines on land and sea across the range of military operations. Employing and countering obstacles differ on land and at sea. For example, while obstacles on land are primarily employed and countered by combat engineers, this is not the case at sea, where ships, aircraft, and underwater elements deploy and/or counter obstacles, naval mines, and IEDs.

The Role of Obstacles in Joint Operations

Employing and countering obstacles impacts (or is impacted by) all six of the **joint functions. Command and control (C2)** is critical to ensure that obstacle employment supports the concept of operations (CONOPS), does not violate law or policy, and avoids unintended consequences. **Intelligence** must provide joint forces with as much understanding as possible about obstacles—and about adversaries' capabilities to employ them. The political, social, cultural, and economic environments are critical elements in understanding the operational environment in which obstacles will be used. Joint forces can use obstacles to enhance the effectiveness of **fires** by increasing target acquisition time, creating target-rich environments, and creating vulnerabilities to exploit. Obstacles can also degrade the ability of friendly forces to employ fires by limiting or denying access to areas needed to launch and recover aircraft or areas from which other weapon systems can employ fires. Obstacles can significantly inhibit the **movement and maneuver** of joint forces and threaten their fighting potential and

Throughout the range of military operations, joint forces may encounter, or be required to employ obstacles of any type. They use obstacles offensively and defensively to attack the mobility of adversaries, enhance the effectiveness of friendly fires, deny adversaries the use of terrain, disrupt sustainment operations, and inflict damage to enemy forces.

---

sustainment. Joint forces must assure their mobility, conserve their fighting potential, and protect their ability to provide personnel, logistics, and other support. Joint forces can use obstacles to delay, channel, or stop the movement and maneuver of adversaries or for **protection** against an enemy's assault or against unauthorized access to facilities and bases.

Assured Mobility

Assured mobility is the framework of processes, actions, and capabilities that assure the ability of the joint force to deploy and maneuver where and when desired, without interruption or delay, to achieve the mission.

Obstacle Framework

Obstacles can be either natural or man-made (or a combination of both).

Natural obstacles are terrain features, such as rivers, forests, or mountains.

Man-made obstacles can be explosive or nonexplosive. **Nonexplosive obstacles** do not contain explosives (although explosives may be detonated to create the obstacle). They include cultural, constructed, and demolition obstacles. **Explosive obstacles** contain explosives and include **mines, IEDs, UXO,** and other explosive hazards (EHs).

Some obstacles are present as inherent aspects of the terrain and are called **existing obstacles.**

Obstacles that are specifically created as obstacles are sometimes called **reinforcing obstacles.**

The Threat

Joint forces typically encounter obstacles in two physical domains: land and maritime.

Land. Joint forces may encounter obstacles on land across the range of military operations. This is especially true in areas with highly restrictive terrain such as mountains, jungles, or urban areas. Adversaries may make extensive use of obstacles, including mines and IEDs, and a variety of countermeasures to defeat friendly obstacles.

Maritime. Enemy mine emplacement operations may be conducted against friendly ports, harbors, and sea lines of communications. Mines may also be used in other areas vital to US and multinational maritime forces such as amphibious objective areas, fire support, and carrier strike group operating areas. The ease of emplacing mines by ship, aircraft, or submarine presents a valid threat to a commander who must rely on naval support or on seaborne reinforcement and resupply.

Air. Control of airspace is essential to effective surface operations. The enemy could emplace nonexplosive obstacles to hamper or impede friendly air maneuver. Cables, balloons, high power transmission line towers (painted to make them difficult to see by friendly air crews) are a couple of examples. Scatterable mines could seriously disrupt and delay air base launch and recovery operations, disrupt logistics sustainment operations to the air base, and thereby limit friendly air operations.

Legal Considerations

The use of some obstacles, specifically mines, is governed by international and US laws and US policies. The United States regards mines as lawful weapons when employed in accordance with accepted legal standards. US policy also governs some demining operations.

Joint Planning Considerations

Authorities and Responsibilities

The President and Secretary of Defense (SecDef) promulgate policy and guidance concerning the employment of mines and humanitarian mine actions (HMAs).

The Secretary of State and ambassadors obtain permission from host nation for employment of mines within their territories or waters.

The Chairman of the Joint Chiefs of Staff transmits policy and guidance concerning the employment of mines and HMAs from the President and SecDef to the combatant commanders.

Joint force commanders (JFCs) provide guidance and direction with respect to employment of barriers, obstacles, and mines.

General Considerations

Barrier, Obstacle, and Minefield Levels of Employment Strategic Employment. Before hostilities, barriers, obstacles, and minefields can be used as flexible deterrent options without posing an offensive threat. Should deterrence fail, offensive maritime mining of enemy ports and waters can constrict enemy seaborne economic war sustainment efforts and reduce enemy ability to safely deploy maritime forces. Similarly, offensive employment of scatterable mines can deny or restrict enemy strategic mobility and sustainability efforts.

Operational Employment. Defensive barrier, obstacle, and minefield employment can help protect friendly ports, lines of communications, and key facilities and free combat forces for offensive employment and denial operations. Offensive employment can protect friendly maneuver while disrupting the enemy's ability to concentrate or maneuver forces.

Tactical Employment. The employment of barriers, obstacles, and minefields at the tactical level is normally done to achieve offensive or defensive objectives to include enhancement of friendly direct/indirect fires, delay/destroy enemy formations, or as an economy of force technique.

To maximize the effectiveness from an operational barrier, obstacle, or minefield, certain factors must be considered.

Placement Considerations. On land, barriers, obstacles, and minefields are usually formed around or tied into an existing terrain feature (e.g., mountain chain or strait) or formed around a man-made structure (e.g., air base, canal, highway, or bridge). At sea, the placement of minefields is usually determined by environmental considerations such as depth, bottom characteristics, and littoral geography. The effects that these operational barriers, obstacles, and minefields will have on both the friendly and enemy forces' ability to maneuver on land and sea or to conduct effective air operations must be analyzed. Reinforcement is achieved by integrating systems of barriers, obstacles, minefields, and fires.

Offensive. The purpose of offensive barrier, obstacle, and minefield employment (to include air-delivered scatterable mines) is to impede or prohibit enemy movements while enhancing or protecting friendly force's maneuverability through or around.

Defensive. The purpose of defensive barrier, obstacle, and minefield emplacement is to degrade the enemy's ability to maneuver, defeat the enemy attack, regain initiative, gain time, concentrate forces, control terrain, and exhaust the enemy prior to assuming the offensive.

Denial Considerations. A denial measure is an action to hinder or deny the enemy the use of territory, personnel, or facilities.

Political and Psychological. The primary objective of employing barriers, obstacles, and minefields may be deterrence rather than physical destruction.

Planning Sequence

The joint operation planning process underpins planning at all levels and for missions across the full range of military operations.

The initial planning guidance includes the identification of areas or zones that require operational-level barriers, obstacles, or minefields; critical targets or enemy functions for attack; sequencing of barrier, obstacle, and minefield employment and desired effects; logistics priorities; rules of engagement; and the employment of obstacles and minefields to support denial operations.

During course of action determination, the JFC's staff initially assesses the terrain, weather, and climate to identify existing operational-level barriers, obstacles, and limits imposed by expected weather. The need for additional barriers, obstacles, and minefields is identified.

During CONOPS development, the JFC's staff initiates the development of the formal barrier and obstacle plan. When completed, the plan should clearly delineate operational barriers, obstacles, and minefields and their intended effect and potential unintended effects on the campaign or operation.

The JFC reviews and approves the concept of employment for operational barriers, obstacles, and minefields as well as the denial plan which is designed to prevent potential aggressors from the use of certain resources, and/or to deny them access to certain areas.

The barrier, obstacle, and MW plan is published, if required, as an appendix of an annex to the theater campaign plan, operation plan, or operation order.

Planning Support

Intelligence. Planning for operations involving barrier, obstacle, and MW requires timely, continuous, and reliable all-source counterintelligence and intelligence support. For each potential operation, analysts must evaluate types, quantities, and capabilities of mines, barriers, and obstacles available to the adversary.

Logistics. Planning for the use of barriers, obstacles, and mines involves the acquisition, storage, maintenance, distribution, and security of the materiel.

Communications. Planning for and employment of barriers, obstacles, and mines requires communication to facilitate joint and multinational coordination and information flow to inform friendly forces (and, when necessary, other government agencies, intergovernmental organizations, and nongovernmental organizations, as well as civilians) of locations.

Explosive Hazards Database. The joint force should establish a single EHs database for the entire operational area to facilitate a common understanding within the joint force and with multinational forces, other government agencies, intergovernmental organizations, and nongovernmental organizations. This database should include all known and suspected mines, IEDs, UXO, and other EHs and be compatible with common operational picture tools to enhance situational awareness and support situational understanding.

Land Operations

Barriers, obstacles, and land mines continue to be a condition in the environment in which land operations are conducted. The condition is significant across the range of military operations; from civil support in an area littered with hurricane debris, through stability operations in which insurgents employ

Scatterable Mines and Networked Munitions. The employment of scatterable mines and networked munitions requires close coordination between components during both the planning and employment phases of the operation. The coordination for the employment of scatterable mines and networked munitions is a combined effort of the joint targeting coordination board, the joint force engineer, and the joint force air component commander, if established. Coordination is essential if scatterable mines or networked munitions are deployed where friendly forces may be operating or in locations that lie within the operational area. Once emplaced, scatterable mines or networked munitions remain active until detonated or until the mines self-destruct or self-deactivate after a preset period of time.

explosive hazards, to offensive or defensive operations employing complex man-made and natural obstacle systems.

Support to Movement and Maneuver. The focus is on supporting the maneuver commander's ability to gain a position of advantage in relation to the enemy; conducting mobility operations to negate the impact of enemy obstacles, conducting countermobility to impact and shape enemy maneuver, or a combination of both. While support to movement and maneuver provides the broader framework of enabling capabilities, the discussion of barriers, obstacles, and MW focuses specifically on mobility and countermobility (and the supporting survivability) tasks.

Engineer Functions. Countering barriers, obstacles, and mines is included within **mobility operations.** The employment of barriers, obstacles, and scatterable mines/networked munitions is included within **countermobility operations.** At the tactical level, mobility and countermobility operations are typically supported by combat engineers as **combat engineering** tasks, although selected combat engineering tasks may also be performed by general engineers.

Mobility Considerations

Mobility operations include five functional areas, three [breaching operations, clearing operations, and gap crossing operations] of which are designed directly to meet challenges from barriers, obstacles, land mines, and other EHs.

Conduct Combined Arms Breaching Operations: detect, breach or bypass, mark, and proof mined areas and obstacles. Combined arms breaching operations are typically performed in a close combat environment.

Conduct Clearing Operations: employ tactics and equipment to detect and eliminate obstacles, mines, and other EHs. Clearing operations are conducted to completely eliminate obstacles, whether along a route or in a specified area.

Conduct Gap Crossing Operations: fill/cross gaps in the terrain/man-made structures to allow personnel and equipment to pass. Gap crossing operations are conducted to project combat power over linear obstacles or gaps.

Countermobility Considerations

Terrain Considerations. Engineers must discern and identify patterns and plan specific detection strategies

The objective of barrier, obstacle, and mine warfare employment is to disrupt, fix, turn, or block enemy forces and protect friendly forces.

based on the threat. The proliferation of mines and IEDs requires engineers to continually develop new countering procedures. The integration of explosive ordnance disposal capabilities into route or area clearance engineer units has become an increasing requirement.

Countermobility Employment Principles Include:

- Barriers, obstacles, and minefields should be evaluated from both an offensive and a defensive posture.

- Barriers, obstacles, and minefields should directly support the maneuver plan.

- Reinforcing obstacles should be integrated with existing barriers and obstacles to support the commander's intent and operational concept.

- Barriers, obstacles, and minefields are more effective when employed in depth.

- By varying the type, design, and location of reinforcing obstacles, the enemy's breaching operation is made more difficult.

- The effectiveness of barrier, obstacle, and mine employment can be affected by the air situation.

- Coverage by observation and by direct or indirect fire is essential to restrict enemy breaching efforts, maneuver, and massing of forces and to increase the destruction of enemy forces.

Command and Control (C2)

Planning. Commanders and staffs consider both friendly and enemy use of obstacles when planning operations.

Reconnaissance. Tactical reconnaissance supporting mobility operations should focus on obstacle intelligence—those collection efforts conducted to detect the presence of enemy (and natural) obstacles, determine their types and dimensions, and provide the necessary information to plan appropriate combined arms breaching, clearance, or bypass operations to negate the impact on the friendly scheme of maneuver.

Control Means. The purpose of obstacle control is to

synchronize subordinate obstacle efforts with the commander's intent and scheme of maneuver. Commanders exercise obstacle control by granting or withholding obstacle emplacement authority or restricting obstacles through orders or other specific guidance.

Reporting, Recording, and Marking. Intelligence concerning enemy minefields is reported by the fastest means available. Spot reports are the tactical commander's most common source of minefield intelligence. Lane or bypass marking is a critical component of obstacle reduction. Effective lane marking allows commanders to project forces through an obstacle quickly, with combat power and C2 intact. It gives an assault force and follow-on forces confidence in the safety of the lane and helps prevent unnecessary casualties.

Maritime Operations

General Discussion

Maritime MW consists of the strategic, operational, and tactical employment of sea mines and mine countermeasures (MCM). MW is divided into two categories: the emplacement of mines to degrade the enemy's capabilities to wage land, air, and maritime warfare; and the countering of enemy mining capability or emplaced mines in order to permit friendly maneuver.

Mine Warfare C2

JFC. Naval MW is an enabler of joint force operations. The JFC is supported in MW by the Navy component commander (NCC), or if assigned, a combined or joint force maritime component commander (JFMCC).

NCC or JFMCC. The NCC or JFMCC staff supports the JFC with all operational-level military operations at sea, including MW. As such, the NCC staff should integrate MW into their planning. The Naval Mine and Anti-Submarine Warfare Command (NMAWC) maintains a deployable staff to provide phased, scalable MW expertise and support to NCCs.

Mine Warfare Commander (MIWC). The MIWC is a supporting warfare commander to the NCC or the officer in tactical command and is the commander's primary advisor on all aspects of MW—both mining and MCM. NMAWC can serve as the MIWC and perform the MW functions in support of the NCC.

Mine Countermeasures Commander (MCMC). The MCMC is the supporting commander to the MIWC or designated commander for MCM within an assigned area. The MCMC controls the operations of MCM assets (surface MCM vessels, airborne MCM [AMCM] squadrons/detachments, and underwater MCM [UMCM] elements) in the operational area.

Environmental Considerations

Environmental considerations are significant in MW and affect both mining and MCM. Mine cases, mine sensors, target signals, and MCM systems are all impacted by environmental factors and impact the selection of equipment and procedures.

Elements of Mine Warfare

MW can be applied across the range of military operations and can be divided into the subdisciplines of mining and MCM.

Mining

Mining is used to support the broad tasks of establishing and maintaining control of essential sea areas. Mining embraces all methods whereby naval mines are used to deny sea area or inflict damage on adversary shipping to hinder, disrupt, and deny adversary operations.

Mine Countermeasures

MCM includes all actions undertaken to prevent enemy mines from altering friendly forces' maritime plans, operations, or maneuver. MCM reduces the threat of mines and the effects of enemy-emplaced sea mines on friendly naval force and seaborne logistics force access to and transit of selected waterways.

Service Considerations

Army–Navy. Naval MW includes mining and MCM in all sea areas, the littoral operating area in an amphibious operation to include the surf zone (SZ) and the beach (as determined in the amphibious planning process), and in certain cases may extend inland where waters are navigable from the sea. In short, if maritime assets are capable of conducting MCM in any waterway where Army craft need to navigate, it is likely that the maritime component commander will be directed to clear those mines.

Air Force–Navy. The United States Air Force (USAF) plays two important roles in supporting MW forces (in addition to supporting offensive MCM). USAF bomber aircraft can deliver large quantities of mines per sortie at long distances from their bases, playing a critical part in accomplishing mining plans directed by joint commands. USAF strike platforms are also a key component of the assault breaching system in support of amphibious operations. The second USAF role is the Air Mobility Command's (AMC's) deployment of AMCM and UMCM forces, and MW C2 elements and the continuing delivery of critical repair parts via AMC aircraft.

Marine Corps–Navy. During amphibious operations, MCM at sea—whether in the deep or shallow water where amphibious ships and their escorts operate, or in the very shallow water and SZ where assault craft bring troops and weapons to the beach—is conducted by a Navy MCMC. Normally, the MCMC is a subordinate and supporting commander to the commander, amphibious task force.

United States Coast Guard (USCG). Coast Guard area commanders are empowered to assign appropriate USCG forces to the JFMCC to support MW operations. USCG assets will likely support route survey and MCM forces conducting MW operations in US territorial waters in times of conflict.

CONCLUSION

This publication provides doctrinal guidance for planning and executing barrier, obstacle, and MW for joint operations as they relate to strategic, operational, and tactical mobility and countermobility across the range of military operations.

Intentionally Blank

CHAPTER I
INTRODUCTION

"Everything that is shot or thrown at you or dropped on you in war is most unpleasant, but of all horrible devices, the most terrifying…is the land mine."

Sir William Slim, Unofficial History, 1959

1. Introduction

a. Joint forces should be prepared to encounter barriers, obstacles (including improvised explosive devices [IEDs], mines, and other unexploded explosive ordnance [UXO]) and to conduct mine warfare (MW), employing mines on land and sea across the range of military operations. In many types of operations, joint forces can employ obstacles as a significant force multiplier.

b. Employing and countering obstacles differ on land and at sea. For example, while obstacles on land are primarily employed and countered by combat engineers, this is not the case at sea, where ships, aircraft, and underwater elements deploy and/or counter obstacles, naval mines, and IEDs. This chapter establishes the basic framework and context for employing and countering obstacles. Considerations that are unique to the land and maritime domains are covered in Chapter III, "Land Operations," and Chapter IV, "Maritime Operations."

2. Operational Framework

a. **The Role of Obstacles in Joint Operations**

(1) Throughout the **range of military operations,** joint forces may encounter, or be required to employ obstacles of any type. In any type of offensive or defensive operation, obstacles can help joint forces to protect personnel, equipment, and facilities and maintain our lines of communications (LOCs). Joint forces conducting **military engagement, security cooperation, and deterrence** activities sometimes use obstacles to enhance deterrence and demonstrate resolve. (In some cases, though, the use of obstacles constitutes an act of war.) In operations such as humanitarian and civic assistance, the very purpose of the operation might be focused on the reduction or elimination of obstacles. Such obstacles may have been emplaced years prior to the operation or by someone other than a current adversary. In **major operations and campaigns,** and some **crisis response and limited contingency operations,** joint forces will be involved in armed conflict. They use obstacles offensively and defensively to attack the mobility of adversaries, enhance the effectiveness of friendly fires, deny adversaries the use of terrain, disrupt sustainment operations, and inflict damage to enemy forces.

(2) Employing and countering obstacles impacts (or is impacted by) all six of the **joint functions. Command and control (C2)** is critical to ensure that obstacle employment supports the concept of operations (CONOPS), does not violate law or policy, and avoids

unintended consequences. Obstacles are a part of the operational environment that can have significant impacts on joint forces. **Intelligence** must provide joint forces with as much understanding as possible about obstacles—and about adversaries' capabilities to employ them. The political, social, cultural, and economic environments are critical elements in understanding the operational environment in which obstacles will be used. Joint forces can use obstacles to enhance the effectiveness of **fires** by increasing target acquisition time, creating target-rich environments, and creating vulnerabilities to exploit. Obstacles can also degrade the ability of friendly forces to employ fires by limiting or denying access to areas needed to launch and recover aircraft or areas from which other weapon systems can employ fires. Obstacles can significantly inhibit the **movement and maneuver** of joint forces and threaten their fighting potential and **sustainment.** Joint forces must assure their mobility, conserve their fighting potential, and protect their ability to provide personnel, logistics, and other support. They do this by predicting and preventing enemy use of obstacles, detecting their existence, avoiding them, neutralizing them, and protecting against their effects. Joint forces can use obstacles to delay, channel, or stop the movement and maneuver of adversaries or for **protection** against an enemy's assault or against unauthorized access to facilities and bases.

(3) Obstacle employment can create significant advantages for the joint forces within the operational area. Likewise, obstacle employment can also create challenges that require consideration prior to emplacement:

(a) The creation and removal of obstacles is often manpower-intensive, hazardous, and can consume a significant amount of time, materiel, equipment, and transportation resources.

(b) Obstacles must be protected to prevent adversaries from bypassing, breaching, or clearing them.

(c) To create certain effects (i.e., disrupt, fix, turn, and block), obstacles require surveillance and dedicated fires.

(d) Obstacles can be just as hazardous to friendly forces and civilians as they are to adversaries. Explosive obstacles must be rendered safe following their operational usefulness.

(e) Obstacles are designed to inhibit the mobility of both enemy and friendly forces.

(f) Employment can have an adverse effect on the perception of mission validity and undermine popular support.

(g) Employment can have an adverse effect on local commerce and can have political and psychological impacts detrimental to stability operations and counterinsurgency operations.

b. **Assured Mobility.** Assured mobility is the framework of processes, actions, and capabilities that assure the ability of the joint force to deploy and maneuver where and when desired, without interruption or delay, to achieve the mission. This construct is one means of enabling a joint force to achieve the commander's intent. Assured mobility emphasizes proactive mobility and countermobility (and supporting survivability) actions and integrates all of the engineer functions to accomplish these actions. Assured mobility should not be confused with the limited application of the mobility function. While focused primarily on the joint function of movement and maneuver, assured mobility has linkages to each of the joint functions and both enables and is enabled by those functions. While the engineer has the primary staff role in assured mobility, other staff members support assured mobility and have critical roles to play. Ultimately, assured mobility is the commander's responsibility. The fundamentals of assured mobility are:

(1) **Predict.** Engineers and planners must accurately predict potential enemy impediments to joint force mobility by analyzing the enemy's tactics, techniques, procedures (TTP), capability, and evolution. Prediction requires a constantly updated understanding of the operational environment. Through the use of joint intelligence preparation of the operational environment (JIPOE), which is designed to be used at the operational level while intelligence preparation of the battlespace (IPB) is a process used by individual commanders within a joint task force to analyze their individual areas of responsibility at the tactical level. JIPOE generally differs from IPB in terms of its relative purpose, focus, and level of detail. While a joint force commander (JFC) will utilize JIPOE to estimate the adversary's overall intent and capability to counter the friendly joint mission, IPB is specifically designed to support the individual ground/naval operations.

(2) **Detect.** Using intelligence, surveillance, and reconnaissance assets, engineers and planners identify the location of natural and man-made obstacles, preparations to create/emplace obstacles, and potential means for obstacle creation. They identify both actual and potential obstacles and propose solutions and alternate courses of action (COAs) to minimize or eliminate their potential impact.

(3) **Prevent.** Engineers and other planners apply this fundamental by denying the enemy's ability to influence mobility. This is accomplished by enacting proactive measures before the obstacles are emplaced or activated. This may include aggressive action to destroy enemy assets/capabilities before they can be used to create obstacles.

(4) **Avoid.** If prevention fails, the commander will maneuver forces to avoid impediments to mobility, if this is viable within the scheme of maneuver.

(5) **Neutralize.** Engineers and other planners plan to neutralize, reduce, or overcome obstacles/impediments as soon as possible to allow unrestricted movement of forces. The breaching tenets and fundamentals apply to the fundamental of "neutralize."

(6) **Protect.** Engineers and other elements plan and implement survivability and other protection measures that will deny the enemy the ability to inflict damage as joint forces maneuver. Protection may include countermobility missions to deny the enemy maneuver and provide protection to friendly maneuvering forces.

(7) **Respond.** Overarching objective of response actions are upon saving lives and maintaining mission capability. Response must be scalable, flexible, and adaptable to operational capabilities, including a well-developed public information and information operations (IO) component. Effective response hinges upon well-trained leaders and personnel who have invested in response preparedness and training. Response will depend on the amount and kind of damage caused by the incident and resources that can be applied.

c. **Obstacle Framework.** Obstacles can be either natural or man-made (or a combination of both), as shown in Figure I-1.

(1) **Natural obstacles** are terrain features, such as rivers, forests, or mountains.

(2) **Man-made obstacles** can be explosive or nonexplosive.

(a) **Nonexplosive obstacles** do not contain explosives (although explosives may be detonated to create the obstacle). They include:

<u>1</u>. **Cultural obstacles** are man-made terrain features that were not created for the purpose of obstructing military forces. Examples include archaeological sites, industrial/commercial infrastructure, major roads and electrical grid components, towns, canals, and railroad embankments.

<u>2</u>. **Constructed obstacles** are created without the use of explosives. Examples include wire obstacles and anti-vehicle ditches.

<u>3</u>. **Demolition obstacles** are created by the detonation of explosives. Examples include bridge demolition, road craters, and abatis.

(b) **Explosive obstacles** contain explosives and include **mines, IEDs, UXO,** and other explosive hazards (EHs).

For additional information about IEDs, see Joint Publication (JP) 3-15.1, Counter-Improvised Explosive Device Operations.

(3) Some obstacles are present as inherent aspects of the terrain and are called **existing obstacles.** Natural and cultural obstacles comprise this category.

(4) Obstacles that are specifically created as obstacles are sometimes called **reinforcing obstacles.** This category includes constructed obstacles, demolition obstacles, IEDs, and mines.

3. The Threat

Joint forces typically encounter obstacles in two physical domains: land and maritime. However, obstacle warfare can impact, and be impacted by, operations in other portions of the operational area.

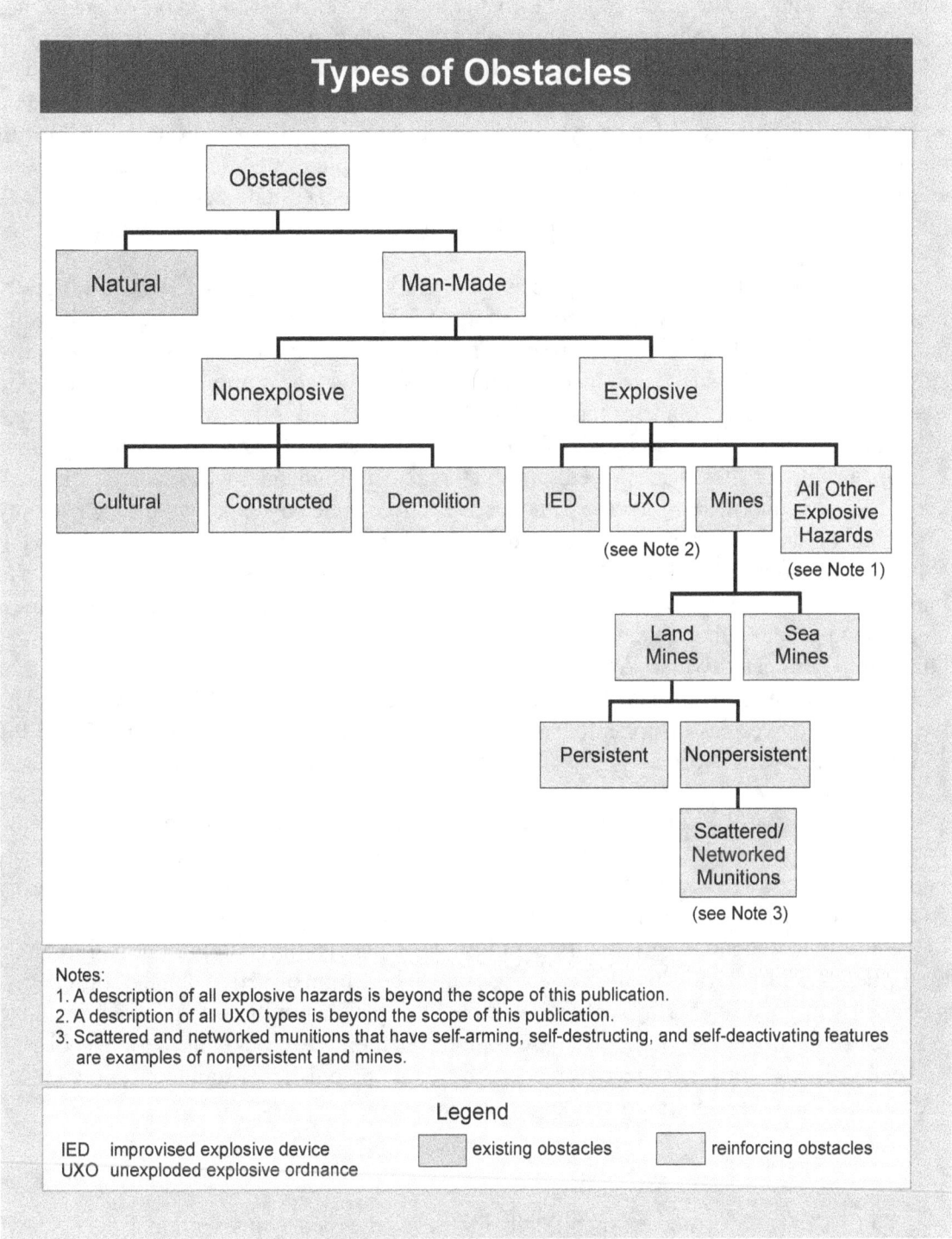

Figure I-1. Types of Obstacles

a. **Land.** Joint forces may encounter obstacles on land across the range of military operations. This is especially true in areas with highly restrictive terrain such as mountains, jungles, or urban areas. Joint forces may face adversaries with highly mobile conventional forces supported by lethal air and ground fires. Enemy surveillance capabilities may determine the effectiveness of employing friendly obstacles. The timing and methods of emplacement may be determined by the air situation. Adversaries may make extensive use of obstacles, including mines and IEDs, and a variety of countermeasures to defeat friendly obstacles. Joint forces may encounter both modern and technologically obsolete mines. The relatively low cost of mines and IEDs and their worldwide availability makes them an ideal weapon for all nations and for anyone with access to them. In addition, enemy use of nuclear munitions and chemical mines should not be ruled out. The threat of terrorist employment of mines, explosives, and booby traps may necessitate defensive measures to reduce the vulnerability of United States (US) personnel, equipment, and facilities.

b. **Maritime.** Enemy mine emplacement operations may be conducted against friendly ports, harbors, and sea lines of communications (SLOCs). Mines may also be used in other areas vital to US and multinational maritime forces such as amphibious objective areas, fire support, and carrier strike group operating areas. The application of technology by industrially advanced countries has produced a sophisticated, effective form of maritime MW. Nevertheless, older mine technologies remain effective. The ease of emplacing mines by ship, aircraft, or submarine presents a valid threat to a commander who must rely on naval support or on seaborne reinforcement and resupply. Maritime power projection and resupply forces originate from friendly ports. During amphibious operations, assault and assault follow-on shipping must transit narrows and operate in shallow waters. The enemy can place these forces at risk, with little cost to its own forces, by emplacing only a few mines. Vessels in port are vulnerable to mines attached to their hulls or other forms of underwater attack by swimmers/divers. Another means of attack while in port or during transits of SLOCs or narrows is by means of suicide and non-suicide waterborne IEDs (WBIEDs). The use of such devices has been demonstrated by al Qaeda in attacks on USS COLE and the Motor/Vessel LIMBURG.

c. **Air.** Control of airspace is essential to effective surface operations. The enemy could emplace nonexplosive obstacles to hamper or impede friendly air maneuver. Cables, balloons, high power transmission line towers (painted to make them difficult to see by friendly air crews) are a couple of examples. Enemy use of mines could pose a major threat to the ability to conduct effective air operations. The enemy might employ sea mines in an area where aircraft carriers would need to operate to be within effective range of the enemy. The enemy might also employ scatterable mines, along with munitions that have immediate effects, in attacks against friendly air bases ashore. Scatterable mines could seriously disrupt and delay air base launch and recovery operations, disrupt logistics sustainment operations to the air base, and thereby limit friendly air operations.

4. Legal Considerations

The use of some obstacles, specifically mines, is governed by international and US laws and US policies. The United States regards mines as lawful weapons when employed in accordance with accepted legal standards. US policy also governs some demining operations. In conducting mining operations, joint forces use the Chairman of the Joint Chiefs of Staff (CJCS) standing rules of engagement in the development of the rules of engagement (ROE) to ensure their actions are consistent with such laws and policies. These laws and policies are complex and occasionally change, so it is critical that joint forces carefully consider them when developing their local ROE and ensure staff judge advocates review them for legal sufficiency. All commanders and staff involved with MW should be familiar with the specific ROE concerning mines. This section identifies the laws, agreements, and policies that are most significant to the employment and counteremployment of obstacles.

a. **International Law.** International law and practice regulate the initiation and conduct of armed conflict, limiting the use of certain types of weapons.

(1) The **law of armed conflict,** also called the law of war, is that part of international law that regulates the conduct of armed hostilities. It postulates four principles: **military necessity, the avoidance of unnecessary suffering, proportionality, and discrimination or distinction.**

(2) **The Hague Conventions.** Commencing in 1899, signatories to the various Hague Conventions sought agreements providing, among others things, regulations for the commencement of hostilities, the conduct of belligerents and neutral powers towards each other and other nations, and limiting the use of certain types of weapons in warfare. The Hague Convention VIII of 1907 addressed contact sea mines and sought to restrict and regulate their use. The relevant provisions of Hague VIII are summarized in Figure I-2.

(3) **International Agreements.** There are two international agreements that bear indirectly on maritime MW.

(a) The **Seabed Arms Control Treaty of 1971** prohibits placing nuclear weapons and other weapons of mass destruction (WMD) on the seabed or subsoil thereof beyond a 12-mile coastal zone. WMD other than nuclear weapons are not defined in this arms control treaty.

(b) The navigation and exclusive economic zone overflight provisions of the 1982 United Nations (UN) Convention on the Law of the Sea (UNCLOS) reflect customary international law and codify the rights and duties of nations with respect to the use of the ocean. Though the US has not ratified UNCLOS, US policy is to consider all navigation and overflight provisions of UNCLOS except those germane to Part XI (deep sea mineral resources) as reflective of international law and, thus, binding on US forces. Mine emplacement operations must consider the applicability of international law and the rights and freedoms enjoyed by all nations.

(4) **The UN Charter** requires member states to refrain from the threat or use of force against the territorial integrity or political independence of any state, except in two situations: individual or collective self-defense and as authorized by the UN Security Council or other competent regional organizations.

(5) **The 1980 United Nations Convention on Prohibitions or Restrictions on the Use of Certain Conventional Weapons Which May be Deemed to be Excessively Injurious or to Have Indiscriminate Effects,** commonly referred to as the 1980 United Nations **Convention on Conventional Weapons (CCW),** is a law of war treaty governing the use of certain conventional weapons which may be deemed to be excessively injurious or to have indiscriminate effects. The US has fully integrated the CCW into land mine doctrine

The Hague Convention (VIII) Provisions

Some of the provision are:

Article 1

It is forbidden—

1. To lay unanchored automatic contact mines, except when they are so constructed as to become harmless one hour at most after the person who laid them ceases to control them;

2. To lay anchored automatic contact mines which do not become harmless as soon as they have broken loose from their moorings;

Article 2

It is forbidden to lay automatic contact mines off the coast and ports of the enemy, with the sole object of intercepting commercial shipping.

Article 3

When anchored automatic contact mines are employed, every possible precaution must be taken for the security of peaceful shipping. The belligerents undertake to do their utmost to render these mines harmless within a limited time, and, should they cease to be under surveillance, to notify the danger zones as soon as military exigencies permit, by a notice addressed to ship owners, which must also be communicated to the governments through the diplomatic channel.

Article 5

At the close of the war, the contracting powers undertake to do their utmost to remove the mines which they have laid, each power removing its own mines. As regards anchored automatic contact mines laid by one of the belligerents off the coast of the other, their position must be notified to the other party by the power which laid them, and each power must proceed with the least possible delay to remove the mines in its own waters.

Figure I-2. The Hague Convention (VIII) Provisions

and practices. **Protocol II (as amended on 3 May 1996) of the CCW** refers to prohibitions or restrictions on the use of land mines, booby traps, and other devices. The protocol does not apply to the use of antiship mines at sea or in inland waterways. Requirements and restrictions on land mines include: requirements to mark, record, and publicize minefield locations at the conclusion of hostilities; joint operations after cessation of hostilities to remove or render ineffective mines and booby traps; requirements on the use of mines or booby traps in areas containing concentrations of civilians; and prohibition on types of booby traps. A 1996 amendment to Protocol II applies to internal conflicts as well as conflicts between states.

(6) **The Mine Ban Treaty (Ottawa Convention) of 1997, to which the US is not a party,** bans the use, production, transfer, and stockpiling of antipersonnel (AP) land mines (APLs) (to include self-destruct/self-deactivating nonpersistent systems) and came into force

on 1 March 1999. The treaty does not restrict the use of antitank mines or anti-vehicle land mines (AVLs), to include those fitted with antihandling devices (AHDs). (Throughout this publication the term AVL is used to represent any antitank or anti-vehicle mine.) The Ottawa Treaty and national implementing legislation in countries party to the treaty establish legal restrictions that necessitate careful planning with US and partner nations when contemplating any activities related to APLs. This position is under review; however, accession to this treaty would prohibit US military use of certain munitions and impacts on political-military relationships, training, plans, and operations with non-Ottawa parties that have APLs for their national defense. Although not applicable to the US, many nations, including many of our allies, have signed the *Convention on the Prohibition of the Use, Stockpiling, Production, and Transfer of Antipersonnel Mines and on Their Destruction.* The US is committed to eliminating the humanitarian risks posed by all persistent land mines, including the AVLs currently permitted under the Ottawa Treaty.

b. **US Law and Policy**

(1) Land Mines

(a) The primary treaty that restricts US use of mines is amended Protocol II, which amends Protocol II to the Convention on Prohibitions or Restrictions on the Use of Certain Conventional Weapons. Amended Protocol II:

1. Expands the scope of the original Protocol to include internal armed conflicts.

2. Requires that all remotely delivered APLs be equipped with self-destruct devices and backup self-deactivation features (making them "smart" mines).

3. Requires that all non-remotely delivered APLs not equipped with such devices ("dumb" mines) be used within controlled, marked, and monitored minefields. The US, as a matter of policy, has committed itself to not use persistent land mines after 2010.

4. Requires that all APLs be detectable using available technology.

5. Requires that the party emplacing mines assume responsibility to ensure against their irresponsible or indiscriminate use.

6. Provides for means to enforce compliance.

7. Clarifies the use of the M18 Claymore "mine" when used in the tripwire mode. (Claymores used in command-detonated mode are not subject to amended Protocol II's restrictions.) Claymores may be used in the tripwire mode without invoking the above "dumb" mine restrictions of amended Protocol II if:

a. They are not left out longer than 72 hours.

<u>b.</u> The Claymores are located in the immediate proximity of the military unit that emplaced them.

<u>c.</u> The area is monitored by military personnel to ensure civilians stay out of the area.

(b) The US land mine policy addresses humanitarian land mine concerns while balancing legitimate warfigher requirements. Under this policy:

<u>1.</u> The policy supports continued use of self-destructing/self-deactivating APLs and AVLs. Self-destructing land mines are not the cause of humanitarian land mine concerns.

<u>2.</u> The US ended the use of persistent land mines of all types at the end of 2010, with the exception of use for mine action/demining training and research purposes.

<u>3.</u> The policy supports the bilateral agreement that directs persistent APLs and AVLs stockpiled in the Republic of Korea (ROK) for use by ROK forces for the defense of the Korean Peninsula may be used but only until the end of 2018.

<u>4.</u> The US no longer uses non-detectable land mines of any type.

(c) CCW Protocol V (Explosive Remnants of War). On 28 November 2003, CCW States Parties adopted Protocol V concerning explosive remnants of war (ERW). It was ratified by the US on 21 January 2009. Protocol V contains no restrictions or prohibitions on weapons or munitions. It addresses what must be done by parties to a conflict with respect to ERW that place civilians at risk and post-conflict remediation. Its focus is on pre-conflict preventive measures and post-conflict corrective measures. Its Technical Annex suggests "best practices" that parties are encouraged to follow on a voluntary basis to achieve greater munitions reliability. Obligations concerning clearance, removal, destruction, recording, precautions, and cooperation and assistance related to ERW apply only to ERW created after entry into force of Protocol V for the state party on whose territory the ERW are located; that is, the obligations are not retroactive.

For additional information on the employment of mines by US forces, refer to Field Manual (FM) 3-100.38/Marine Corps Reference Publication (MCRP) 3-17.2B/Navy Tactics, Techniques, and Procedures (NTTP) 3-02.4.1/Air Force Tactics, Techniques, and Procedures (Instruction) (AFTTP[I]) 3-2.12, UXO-Multi-Service Tactics, Techniques, and Procedures for Unexploded Explosive Ordnance Operations; *Navy Warfare Publication (NWP) 3-15,* Naval Mine Warfare; *Marine Corps Warfighting Publication (MCWP) 5-12.1/NWP 1-14M/Commandant of the Coast Guard Publication P5800.7A,* The Commander's Handbook on the Law of Naval Operations *(section 7.7 and 9.2); and FM 4-30.51/MCRP 3-17.2A,* Unexploded Ordnance (UXO) Procedures.

(2) **US Policy on Humanitarian Demining.** The US Humanitarian Mine Action Program has supported and funded humanitarian demining (HDM) efforts since 1988. Because of the threat to peace and safety, HDM operations have become a significant disarmament and peace operations activity. Demining is ultimately a host nation (HN)

responsibility; however, the US promotes its foreign policy interests by assisting other nations in protecting their populations from land mines through mine awareness education and training of HN personnel in the surveying, marking, and clearing of mines. While providing such assistance US military forces are prohibited from engaging in the physical detection, lifting, or destroying of land mines, except in limited circumstances. See Appendix F, "Humanitarian Mine Action;" JP 3-34, *Joint Engineer Operations;* and JP 3-29, *Foreign Humanitarian Assistance*, for additional information.

Intentionally Blank

CHAPTER II
JOINT PLANNING CONSIDERATIONS

"Battles are won through the ability of men to express concrete ideas in clear and unmistakable language."

Brigadier General S.L.A. Marshall
US Army (1900–1977)

1. Authorities and Responsibilities

a. The President of the United States and the Secretary of Defense (SecDef)

(1) **Mine Release Authority. The authority to employ mines originates with the President.** Since the employment of mines in international waters or in foreign territories (including territorial seas) is generally a hostile act, the President must authorize them. Employing mines in allied territory or waters is permissible with HN permission and Presidential authorization. US joint forces will only employ nonpersistent mines: those that are capable of self-destruction and/or self-deactivation.

(2) **The President and SecDef:**

(a) Approve ROE established by the geographic combatant commander (GCC) for the theater.

(b) Promulgate policy and guidance concerning the employment of mines and humanitarian mine actions (HMAs).

b. The Secretary of State and ambassadors obtain permission from HN for employment of mines within their territories or waters.

c. CJCS

(1) Issues standing ROE.

(2) Transmits policy and guidance concerning the employment of mines and HMAs from the President and SecDef to the combatant commanders (CCDRs).

d. JFCs

(1) **CCDRs**

(a) Augment ROE (with approval by the President and SecDef as required).

(b) Distribute ROE to subordinate and subordinate commands for compliance.

(c) Provide guidance and direction with respect to employment of barriers, obstacles, and mines.

(2) **Joint Task Force Commanders**

(a) Request supplemental ROE for MW as required.

(b) Provide guidance and direction with respect to employment of barriers, obstacles, and mines.

2. General Considerations

a. **Barrier, Obstacle, and Minefield Levels of Employment**

(1) **Strategic Employment.** Before hostilities, barriers, obstacles, and minefields can be used as flexible deterrent options without posing an offensive threat. Defensive employment along a hostile land border can demonstrate friendly resolve. Maritime defensive and protective mining can help protect friendly ports and waters. Pre-hostility employment will be as directed by the President. Presidential determination will be based, in part, on diplomatic conditions and on concurrence by affected friendly nations. Should deterrence fail, offensive maritime mining of enemy ports and waters can constrict enemy seaborne economic war sustainment efforts and reduce enemy ability to safely deploy maritime forces. Similarly, offensive employment of scatterable mines can deny or restrict enemy strategic mobility and sustainability efforts.

(2) **Operational Employment.** Defensive barrier, obstacle, and minefield employment can help protect friendly ports, LOCs, and key facilities and free combat forces for offensive employment and denial operations. Offensive employment can protect friendly maneuver while disrupting the enemy's ability to concentrate or maneuver forces. Barriers and obstacles of operational significance usually differ in scale from those of tactical significance. However, size alone does not make an obstacle operationally significant. At the operational level, the primary use of obstacles is to restrict enemy maneuver options or to create friendly maneuver options. Major natural terrain features and enemy disposition provide the foundation for the development of an obstacle or barrier plan. Operational barriers and obstacles may be created by the composite effect of many closely coordinated tactical obstacles or by the reinforcement of natural obstacles to form large terrain or massive obstacles. An example of a massive obstacle is the temporary flooding caused by the destruction of a major river dam. Mines can also contribute to gaining air superiority. Mines can delay efforts to repair damage to air bases caused by munitions that have immediate effects, thus degrading or denying the base's capability to launch or recover aircraft. Mines can also restrict the deployment of mobile, surface-based air defenses, as well as surface-to-surface systems, because rapid movement in a mined area increases the risk of a mine encounter. Mines can also disrupt logistics sustainment operations being performed in the enemy's rear area.

(3) **Tactical Employment.** The employment of barriers, obstacles, and minefields at the tactical level is normally done to achieve offensive or defensive objectives to include

enhancement of friendly direct/indirect fires, delay/destroy enemy formations, or as an economy of force technique.

b. **Placement Considerations.** To maximize the effectiveness from an operational barrier, obstacle, or minefield, certain factors must be considered.

(1) On land, barriers, obstacles, and minefields are usually formed around or tied into an existing terrain feature (e.g., mountain chain or strait) or formed around a man-made structure (e.g., air base, canal, highway, or bridge). At sea, the placement of minefields is usually determined by environmental considerations such as depth, bottom characteristics, and littoral geography. Although there is little flexibility in positioning these large-scale obstructions, flexibility exists in selecting and designating features that will be enhanced or reinforced. Operational barriers, obstacles, and minefields are placed to manipulate the enemy in such a way that supports the commander's intent and scheme of maneuver and should be observed or covered by fire.

(2) The effects that these operational barriers, obstacles, and minefields will have on both the friendly and enemy forces' ability to maneuver on land and sea or to conduct effective air operations must be analyzed. Effects of obstacles include disrupt, fix, turn, or block enemy forces. Operational barriers, obstacles, and minefields do more than just degrade the maneuver of enemy forces. Because of their size and the pattern of placement, they virtually dictate the maneuver options of both friendly and enemy forces; moreover, they serve to fix opposing maneuver elements within a "target window," thus increasing lethality of supporting arms.

(3) The element of surprise can also be achieved through the employment of barriers, obstacles, and minefields. Because of their operational significance, both friendly and enemy forces usually know of their existence and location. Surprise can result when a barrier, obstacle, or minefield perceived by one force as significant fails to effectively obstruct the opponent. This implies that the operational significance of a barrier, obstacle, or minefield depends both on its physical obstruction capability and the way in which the opposing forces perceive it. Joint forces can achieve surprise through the use of air- or artillery-delivery systems that permit rapid mining in the operational area. These can confront the attacker with a completely new situation almost instantly. The use of hard-to-detect employment means such as submarines is another way to achieve surprise. Surprise can be further gained through the use of lanes and gaps, phony minefields and obstacles, and self-destructing or self-deactivating mines. Friendly forces should avoid readily discernible or repetitive employment methods and utilize deceptive measures. When the type, location, and design are varied, the enemy's understanding and breaching of friendly barriers, obstacles, and minefields is made more difficult.

(4) Tactical barriers, obstacles, and minefields can be used offensively and defensively to help secure the population and provide protection for forward operating bases.

(5) Barriers are also used in humanitarian assistance/disaster relief and civil support operations for population and resource control. Civil affairs (CA) personnel should be

consulted regarding the appropriate use of this capability in these types of operations and the potential impact on local attitudes.

(6) Reinforcement is achieved by integrating systems of barriers, obstacles, minefields, and fires. The objective is to degrade enemy movement, assist counterattacks, and facilitate future friendly offensive operations.

(7) Reinforcing obstacles and minefields are identified as early as possible, because the development of a barrier, obstacle, or minefield system in depth requires time, the commitment of engineer or specialized resources, extensive logistics support, or other forces such as overwatching maneuver elements.

(8) Plans include the identification of assets to restore the integrity of a barrier, obstacle, or minefield if breached by the enemy. This is especially important if the obstruction is critical to operational success.

(9) In operations involving land forces, the creation of massive obstacles should be considered in situations where friendly forces control a major river dam. Control of the dam provides the option of limited, controlled flooding or destruction of the dam to create both a destructive flood surge and flooded areas. The same might be applied to the destruction of large bridges that cross substantial watercourses or other large gaps. However, such actions should only be considered after carefully considering the treatment of any such actions under the law of war and the ROE for the operational area. Any commander considering destruction of dams, bridges or other civilian infrastructure must carefully conduct a proportionality analysis with the staff judge advocate to ensure the military gain is significant enough to outweigh the likely impact to civilian personnel and property. Commanders should also coordinate with the public affairs office to enable a coordinated response to any public or media interest in such destruction.

c. **Offensive.** The purpose of offensive barrier, obstacle, and minefield employment (to include air-delivered scatterable mines) is to impede or prohibit enemy movements while enhancing or protecting friendly force's maneuverability through or around. This is achieved by influencing or controlling the movement of enemy ground and naval forces and degrading enemy air bases operations. The enemy's ability to counterattack or reinforce is restricted, and the operational area is isolated. Barriers, obstacles, and mines have five main objectives in offensive operations (see Figure II-1).

(1) **Prevent Enemy Reinforcement or Counterattack.** To prevent the enemy from reinforcing or counterattacking, critical routes are interdicted to hinder movement of reserves and logistics. Speed and depth are vital.

(2) **Facilitate Economy of Force.** Barriers, obstacles, and minefields permit fewer forces to defend selected sectors, thereby allowing relieved maneuver units and other combat resources to be concentrated in other zones for attack. Similarly, they become a combat multiplier, amplifying the firepower effectiveness of the friendly forces defending them by creating optimum fields of fire. Easily defended choke points can be effectively reinforced with obstacles, supported by on-call fire support, and held by relatively small forces.

Barriers, Obstacles, and Minefields Objectives

OFFENSIVE
Enhances and protects the friendly force's ability to maneuver

- Prevent enemy reinforcement or counterattack
- Facilitate economy of force
- Provide security
- Degrade enemy air capability
- Fix the enemy

DEFENSIVE
Directed toward degrading the enemy's ability to maneuver or protect the force

- Destroy or attrit the enemy force
- Support economy of force measures
- Retention of key terrain or areas of significant strategic, operational, or tactical value
- Force protection

Figure II-1. Barriers, Obstacles, and Minefields Objectives

(3) **Provide Security.** Barriers, obstacles, and minefields can be used in critical areas along the flanks of advancing forces to restrict enemy attacks. At the operational level, river systems, mountain ranges, deserts, and snow- or ice-covered areas are natural barriers and obstacles that can enhance flank security. Shallows, reefs, and other maritime hazards can be used at sea. Existing barriers and obstacles can be strengthened with reinforcing obstacles and minefields to counter an enemy threat.

(4) **Degrade Enemy Air Capability.** Mines can pose a significant obstacle to the enemy's ability to recover and resume operations after an air base attack. Any delays in the enemy generating sorties can provide friendly forces with an important opportunity to further suppress the enemy's ability to defend against follow-on attacks, leading to the enemy's loss of control of the air.

(5) **Fix the Enemy.** Air- and artillery-delivered scatterable mines and emplaced mines can disrupt and delay the enemy's retreat during pursuit and exploitation. They can also be used to disrupt the commitment of the enemy's reserve and follow-on forces.

d. **Defensive.** The purpose of defensive barrier, obstacle, and minefield emplacement is to degrade the enemy's ability to maneuver, defeat the enemy attack, regain initiative, gain

A main priority in defense is the degradation of enemy ability to maneuver.

time, concentrate forces, control terrain, and exhaust the enemy prior to assuming the offensive. Naval MW distinguishes between defensive minefields, which are minefields laid in international waters or international straits with the declared intention of controlling shipping in defense of sea communications, and protective minefields, which are minefields laid in friendly territorial waters to protect ports, harbors, anchorages, coasts, and coastal routes. Barriers, obstacles, and mines have four main objectives in defensive operations (see Figure II-1).

(1) **Destroy or Attrit the Enemy Force.** Barriers, obstacles, and mines can enhance the effectiveness of friendly fires or delay the enemy's advance, upset timing, disrupt, and channelize formations, and delay or destroy follow-on forces.

(2) **Support of Economy of Force Measures.** Barriers, obstacles, and mines can be used in the economy of force role to strengthen a naturally strong existing obstacle area so that it need only be lightly defended, thus freeing forces to be concentrated elsewhere. Similarly, obstacles can be used in conjunction with mobile forces to protect flanks and other lightly defended areas.

(3) **Retention or Denial of Key Terrain.** Barriers, obstacles, and mines can be used to deny the enemy access to key terrain or areas of significant strategic, operational, or tactical value.

(4) **Force Protection.** Create barriers and obstacles for force protection.

e. **Denial Considerations.** A denial measure is an action to hinder or deny the enemy the use of territory, personnel, or facilities. It may include destruction, removal, contamination, or erection of obstructions.

(1) The GCC establishes the theater policies governing denial operations in coordination with allied or friendly governments. Detailed planning and execution are subsequently delegated to subordinate commanders. In developing denial policies, consideration must be given to those facilities and areas required to support life in the post-hostility period regardless of the outcome of the conflict. The long-range social, economic, political, and psychological effects of destruction of civil properties and material must be weighed against the military advantages gained. The law of war requires that denial operations be targeted toward the enemy's forces and not be used to cause unnecessary human suffering and physical destruction.

(2) Denial operations usually do not focus upon immediate enemy destruction, but rather on contributing to future friendly operations. Denial operations may have a major impact on the civilian population. Denial targets frequently involve civil facilities and structures, such as electrical power generation facilities and ports, and require careful judgment regarding the military importance versus the impact on the civilian population.

f. **Deception.** Deception is defined as those measures designed to mislead the enemy by manipulation, distortion, or falsification of evidence to induce the enemy to react in a manner prejudicial to enemy interests. There are two basic approaches to deception. The first is to increase uncertainty in order to forestall the enemy's timely reaction. The second is to misdirect the enemy toward a COA that favors friendly operations. Barriers, obstacles, and minefields can support the aims of both approaches. Time and enemy surveillance techniques will determine the best method of employing barriers, obstacles, and minefields in support of deception. Allowing the enemy to observe units or vessels engaged or preparing to engage in seemingly realistic employment or breaching operations transmits a specific message to the enemy. Operations must be planned so that their execution will not inadvertently reveal friendly plans. The employment of phony obstacles and minefields is a deception technique. Allowing the enemy access to manipulated or distorted friendly operation plans (OPLANs) that support observations of friendly activity may significantly enhance the believability of the deception.

See JP 3-13.4, Military Deception.

g. **Political and Psychological.** The primary objective of employing barriers, obstacles, and minefields may be deterrence rather than physical destruction. Accordingly, political and psychological considerations are key aspects that have far-reaching implications. From a political perspective, such measures will signal friendly resolve to take actions required to protect national interests. Psychological deterrence is also achieved. Although the degree of psychological deterrence cannot be quantified, the mere suspicion that mines have been emplaced can adversely affect enemy planning and operations in excess of the actual threat. The psychological impact of mines can be increased by news media exposure of their existence and lack of a ready capability to implement countermeasures. These considerations should be included in the development of the IO portion of the joint operation.

3. Planning Sequence

The joint operation planning process (JOPP) underpins planning at all levels and for missions across the full range of military operations. It applies to both supported and supporting JFCs and to joint force component commands when the components participate in joint planning. The primary steps of JOPP are shown in Figure II-2 and are discussed in the remainder of this section.

a. **Planning Initiation.** JOPP begins when an appropriate authority recognizes a potential for military capability to be employed in response to a potential or actual crisis. At the strategic level, that authority—the President, SecDef, or the CJCS—initiates COA

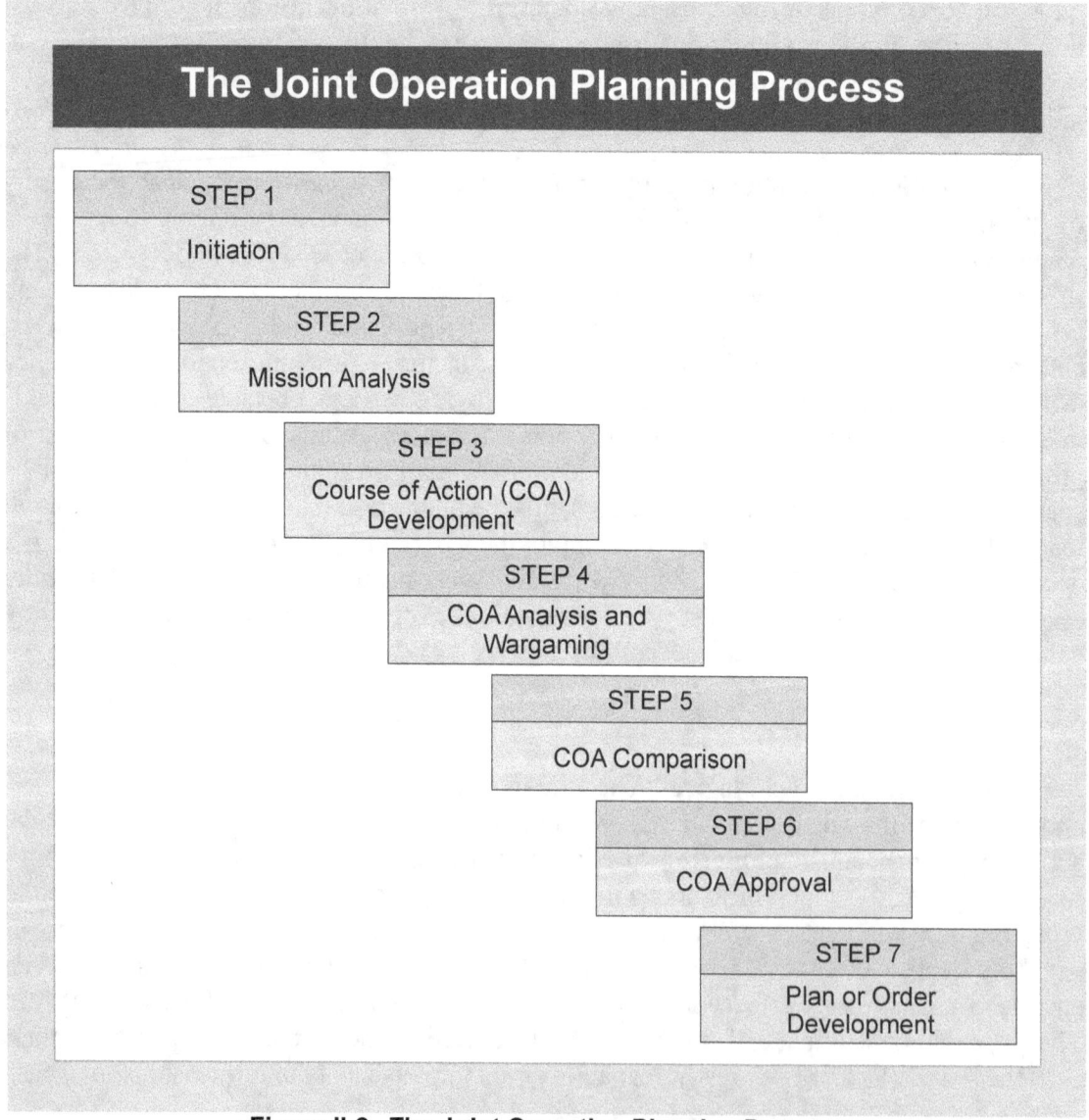

The Joint Operation Planning Process

STEP 1
Initiation

STEP 2
Mission Analysis

STEP 3
Course of Action (COA) Development

STEP 4
COA Analysis and Wargaming

STEP 5
COA Comparison

STEP 6
COA Approval

STEP 7
Plan or Order Development

Figure II-2. The Joint Operation Planning Process

development by deciding to develop military options. In an actual crisis, the CJCS will issue a warning order. CCDRs and other commanders also may initiate COA development on their own authority when they identify a planning requirement not directed by higher authority.

b. **Mission Analysis.** The joint force's mission is the task or set of tasks, together with the purpose, that clearly indicates the action to be taken and the reason for doing so. The primary products of mission analysis are a revised mission statement, the JFC's initial intent statement, initial planning guidance, and the commander's critical information requirements. The initial planning guidance includes the identification of areas or zones that require operational-level barriers, obstacles, or minefields; critical targets or enemy functions for attack; sequencing of barrier, obstacle, and minefield employment and desired effects; logistics priorities; ROE; and the employment of obstacles and minefields to support denial operations.

c. **COA Determination.** COA determination consists of four primary activities: COA development, analysis and wargaming, comparison, and approval. A good COA accomplishes the mission within the commander's guidance and positions the joint force for future operations, and provides flexibility to meet unforeseen events during execution. During COA determination, the JFC's staff initially assesses the terrain, weather, and climate to identify existing operational-level barriers, obstacles, and limits imposed by expected weather. The need for additional barriers, obstacles, and minefields is identified. Areas suitable for enhancement and reinforcement are identified. Special attention is given to identifying areas that could be reinforced to form massive area obstacles. The terrain is evaluated from both friendly and enemy perspectives. The evaluation considers the enemy's ability and willingness to cross difficult terrain. Friendly capabilities should not be assumed to be the same as enemy capabilities. Both friendly and enemy perspectives and capabilities are evaluated to estimate options available to each side. The terrain and climate assessments during the initial stage of the plan development phase will enhance the integration of barriers, obstacles, and minefields into the overall plan. Once the COA is approved, the staff converts the COA into a CONOPS.

d. **Plan or Order Development.** Contingency planning will result in plan development, while crisis action planning will lead directly to operation order (OPORD) development. During plan or order development, the commander and staff, in collaboration with subordinate and supporting components and organizations, expand the approved COA into a detailed joint OPLAN or OPORD by first developing an executable CONOPS. The CONOPS describes how the actions of the joint force components and supporting organizations will be integrated, synchronized, and phased to accomplish the mission, including potential branches and sequels. During CONOPS development, the JFC's staff initiates the development of the formal barrier and obstacle plan. This may include the employment of reinforcing barriers, obstacles, and minefields. Emphasis is placed on maximizing the effectiveness of existing barriers and obstacles. Each barrier and obstacle plan requires an estimate of possible or probable enemy actions to identify opportunities for offensive and defensive action. When completed, the plan should clearly delineate operational barriers, obstacles, and minefields and their intended effects and potential unintended effects on the campaign or operation.

(1) The JFC and staff must consider the various component weapons systems and delivery assets available to deliver or emplace the selected reinforcing barriers, obstacles, and minefields. The delivery or emplacement assets must be identified and allocated accordingly. The JFC is also responsible for integrating this support into the overall campaign or operation.

(2) The barrier and obstacle plan formulation should also identify areas that must remain free of obstacles or minefields to facilitate friendly maneuver. Such areas are necessary to exploit the advantages gained from enemy reactions and vulnerabilities. At the tactical level in ground operations, this is achieved through the designation of obstacle zones and belts.

(3) Although sustainment is a Service component responsibility, the JFC must consider the capabilities, vulnerabilities, and limitations of logistics systems in the planning and execution of the operation. To achieve flexibility, the JFC must anticipate current and future requirements, the potential for degradation by enemy action, and the ability to sustain operations throughout an entire operation or campaign.

(4) The barrier, obstacle, and minefield guidance contained in the OPLAN should provide for the necessary control of obstacle or minefield areas and obstacle or minefield restricted areas. It may designate critical obstacles and reserve the execution of selected obstacles. However, restrictions placed on subordinate commanders should be limited to those deemed necessary by the JFC. At a minimum, guidance should delineate any special reporting, recording, and marking responsibilities.

(5) The development of the joint campaign or OPLAN necessarily includes estimates from the component commanders as to how their assets and capabilities can best support the JFC's objectives.

e. The JFC reviews and approves the concept of employment for operational barriers, obstacles, and minefields as well as the denial plan which is designed to prevent potential aggressors from the use of certain resources, and/or to deny them access to certain areas. As part of this approval process, the JFC verifies that the CONOPS meets intent and guidance and facilitates synchronization to produce the most effective employment of operational barriers, obstacles, and mines.

f. Once formal approval of the OPLAN is obtained, subordinate and supporting commanders develop their own plans. In doing so, they can determine how existing and reinforcing barriers, obstacles, and minefields will affect maneuver, what conditions are imposed on battle plans, and how to employ supporting obstacles. Although this is addressed as a separate step, subordinate and supporting commanders develop plans concurrently with those of the JFC.

g. The barrier, obstacle, and mine warfare plan is published, if required, as an appendix of an annex to the theater campaign plan, OPLAN, or OPORD. In addition, the reporting of execution or employment of barriers, obstacles, and minefields should be addressed in

OPLAN or OPORD annexes and appendices (e.g., ROE and unit standard operating procedure [SOP]).

h. Although employment is addressed separately in this publication, planning and employment is a continuous process. As one operation is executed, the next one is planned, coordinated, and executed. In addition, planners must closely monitor execution and be prepared to adapt the plan, and future plans, in response to changing circumstances. This may involve reapportioning and reallocating assets and reprioritizing support for barrier, obstacle, and minefield emplacement.

i. Plans for the removal or deactivation of mines, barriers, and obstacles may need to be formulated and employed during or after hostilities or other operations.

4. Planning Support

a. **Intelligence.** Planning for operations involving barrier, obstacle, and mine warfare requires timely, continuous, and reliable all-source counterintelligence and intelligence support. Figure II-3 identifies some typical intelligence support tasks. During the planning process, engineers require a variety of intelligence products to include geospatial intelligence (GEOINT) provided by the National Geospatial-Intelligence Agency.

(1) Collection, production, and dissemination of intelligence information must start during peacetime. Tasks include identifying and evaluating worldwide mine production facilities and storage capabilities (to include on-hand quantities). For each potential operation, analysts must evaluate types, quantities, and capabilities of mines, barriers, and obstacles available to the adversary. The evaluation includes technical information on each type of mine (characteristics, description, capability, and vulnerabilities).

(2) JIPOE is a process used to identify adversary mine, barrier, and obstacle storage locations; topographic, hydrographic, and oceanographic information; actual and potential locations of adversary mine, barrier, and obstacle employment; the adversary's doctrine, TTP for countering and employing it; fire support to support mine, barriers, and obstacles (doctrine, capabilities, unit locations); breaching capabilities (assets, doctrine, and TTP); and current and future operational capabilities (see JP 2-01.3, *Joint Intelligence Preparation of the Operational Environment*).

(3) Once conflict begins, intelligence collection (including reconnaissance and combat units) must locate enemy barrier, mine, and obstacle locations; identify and locate enemy fire support; identify remaining enemy employment capabilities; and locate enemy breaching assets. This information, particularly any updates, must be pushed down to tactical echelons. Given known enemy doctrine, TTP, intelligence must advise the JFC as to how the enemy will react to friendly operations.

Doctrine and responsibilities for intelligence support are addressed in JP 2-0, Joint Intelligence.

b. **Logistics.** Planning for the use of barriers, obstacles, and mines involves the acquisition, storage, maintenance, distribution, and security of the materiel. Logistics

Intelligence Support Tasks

Tasks include identifying and evaluating...

- Worldwide mine production capabilities and facilities

- Types, quantities, and capabilities of mines, barriers, and obstacles available

- Technical information on each type of mine (characteristics, description, capability, and vulnerabilities)

- Enemy mine, barrier, and obstacle storage locations

- Topographic, hydrographic, and oceanographic information

- Actual and potential locations for enemy mine, barrier, and obstacle employment

- The enemy's doctrine, tactics, techniques, and procedures for employing mines, barriers, and obstacles

- Enemy fire support for mines, barriers, and obstacles (doctrine, capabilities, unit locations)

- Enemy breaching capabilities (assets, doctrine, and tactics, techniques, and procedures)

- The enemy's current and future operational capabilities

- Increased activity near suspected storage sites indicative of enemy intent to mine

Figure II-3. Intelligence Support Tasks

planners must be included early in the planning process to ensure proper coordination and timely acquisition of the resources that will be needed to execute the plan.

(1) **Acquisition and Storage.** Anticipation is key to a sound acquisition and storage plan. Planners must ensure that the proper mix of mines and minefield, obstacle, and barrier emplacing materials and counterobstacle equipment and materiel are made available in time to meet the demands of the OPLAN. Requirements at the operational level must be anticipated to prevent delays in delivery of the material to a theater. Unless they are special munitions, the storage of mines will normally be handled like any other munitions.

(2) **Distribution.** The execution of this logistics function is crucial to the success of the OPLAN. It helps transform the OPLAN into tactical operations. Logistics planners must ensure the availability of sufficient resources to transport barrier or obstacle material and mines to the place of employment or deployment.

(3) **Legal Concerns.** Because the use, possession, transfers, and stockpiling of land mines is closely regulated under various international agreements and because countries have differing legal obligations related to the possession, use, storage, and transport of land mines, the international movement and storage of mines must be carefully coordinated to avoid legal and political repercussions.

c. **Communications.** Planning for and employment of barriers, obstacles, and mines requires communication to facilitate joint and multinational coordination and information flow to inform friendly forces (and, when necessary, other government agencies, intergovernmental organizations, and nongovernmental organizations, as well as civilians) of locations. These activities require that secure, interoperable communications systems are available to support the mission.

d. **Explosive Hazards Database.** The joint force should establish a single EHs database for the entire operational area to facilitate a common understanding within the joint force and with multinational forces, other government agencies, intergovernmental organizations, and nongovernmental organizations. This database should include all known and suspected mines, IEDs, UXO, and other EHs and be compatible with common operational picture (COP) tools to enhance situational awareness and support situational understanding. The rapid and timely declassification of military data on locations of mines and other EHs is essential for information sharing and development of a COP, which allows friendly forces the ability to safely navigate around or through these known obstacles.

For more information, see JP 5-0, Joint Operation Planning.

Intentionally Blank

CHAPTER III
LAND OPERATIONS

"Gentlemen, I don't know whether we will make history tomorrow, but we will certainly change geography."

**Sir Herbert Plumer (to press conference
the day before the blowing up of
Messines Ridge, 6 June 1917)**

1. General Discussion

Barriers, obstacles, and land mines continue to be a condition in the environment in which land operations are conducted. The condition is significant across the range of military operations; from civil support in an area littered with hurricane debris, through stability operations in which insurgents employ EHs, to offensive or defensive operations employing complex man-made and natural obstacle systems. This chapter discusses the framework for planning and conducting land operations to minimize the impact **from barriers, obstacles, and land mines and to synchronize their employment.**

a. **Scatterable Mines and Networked Munitions.** The employment of scatterable mines and networked munitions requires close coordination between components during both the planning and employment phases of the operation. The coordination for the employment of scatterable mines and networked munitions is a combined effort of the joint targeting coordination board (JTCB), the joint force engineer, and the joint force air component commander (JFACC), if established. The JFACC is responsible for planning and delivery of air-delivered scatterable mines. The planning and integration of minefields into the barrier plan is the responsibility of the joint force engineer. The JTCB is responsible for facilitating joint forces targeting operations by establishing a forum to ensure support and synchronization of JFC objectives as well as integrating and deconflicting all joint force component operations. To ensure a coordinated effort, a general CONOPS is developed that includes such issues as identification of objectives, timing, minefield placement, and ingress or egress routes. Coordination is essential if scatterable mines or networked munitions are deployed where friendly forces may be operating or in locations that lie within the operational area. Once emplaced, scatterable mines or networked munitions remain active until detonated or until the mines self-destruct or self-deactivate after a preset period of time. Required self-destruct or self-deactivate times depend upon the operational or tactical situation and are not necessarily related to the proximity of friendly forces. US scatterable mines and networked munitions are all designed to self-destruct and/or self-deactivate. Scatterable mines and networked munitions are selected when they are the optimum means available to support the JFC's CONOPS.

(1) Employing scatterable mines and networked munitions requires prior coordination with and approval from the commander within whose boundaries the mines are employed. Specific coordination procedures should provide an optimum balance between requirements for control and flexibility in execution. In areas close to friendly forces or

where friendly forces may operate before the mines self-destruct, detailed coordination is essential. Upon approval, the location of employment will be reported by the employing force to the appropriate ground force commander.

(2) Scatterable mines and networked munitions are most effective when combined with other weapons to delay, disrupt, destroy, or turn enemy forces. They can complement organic capabilities. For example, scatterable mines and networked munitions can be used to secure flanks of ground units, close breaches in minefields and obstacles, or protect an amphibious objective area (AOA).

(3) In early stages of contingency operations or at extended ranges, air-deliverable scatterable mines may be the only available mining capability.

(4) Minefields employed in direct support of ground forces have limited effectiveness if unobserved and not covered by some means of fire or fire support.

(5) If scatterable mines are the only type of ordnance that will satisfy the ground force commander's requirements, their use should be specified in the ground force commander's request. Similarly, if employment of scatterable mines in a specified area is not acceptable (i.e., likely to create an undesired effect) this should also be specified in the ground force plan.

b. **Support to Movement and Maneuver.** Support to movement and maneuver is the integrated application of assured mobility throughout the operational area to preserve combat power. It is the framework within which consideration of barriers, obstacles, and mine warfare occurs. Support to movement and maneuver consists of the subtasks, capabilities, and systems within the joint functions that enable both mobility and countermobility operations. The focus is on supporting the maneuver commander's ability to gain a position of advantage in relation to the enemy; conducting mobility operations to negate the impact of enemy obstacles, conducting countermobility to impact and shape enemy maneuver, or a combination of both. Support to movement and maneuver includes more than the capability to employ or counter obstacles. For example, it includes the regulation of traffic in the maneuver space, the handling of displaced persons, and other capabilities to support the maneuver plan. While support to movement and maneuver provides the broader framework of enabling capabilities, the discussion of barriers, obstacles, and mine warfare focuses specifically on mobility and countermobility (and the supporting survivability) tasks. Countermobility and supporting survivability operations are also linked to the joint function of protection since survivability is one of the subordinate tasks of that function.

c. **Engineer Functions.** The three engineer functions are combat, general, and geospatial engineering. Countering barriers, obstacles, and mines is included within **mobility operations.** The employment of barriers, obstacles, and scatterable mines/networked munitions is included within **countermobility operations.** At the tactical level, mobility and countermobility operations are typically supported by combat engineers as **combat engineering** tasks, although selected combat engineering tasks may also be performed by general engineers. Combat engineers are specifically organized, trained, and equipped to perform these tasks in close combat in support of a combined arms force. (For further information about the engineer functions and the differences between combat and general engineers, see JP 3-34, *Joint Engineer Operations.*) The remainder of this chapter discusses those combat engineering mobility, countermobility, and supporting survivability tasks that shape or deny land operational environment by employing or countering the employment of barriers, obstacles, and land mines. General engineering may also support mobility, countermobility, and survivability operations at all levels of war. Geospatial engineering is present to support all engineer operations.

2. Mobility Considerations

a. **General.** Mobility operations include five functional areas, three of which are designed directly to meet challenges from barriers, obstacles, land mines, and other (EHs). These three (breaching operations, clearing operations, and gap crossing operations) are discussed further in paragraphs b through d below. The five functional areas of mobility operations for Army units and Marine air-ground task forces (MAGTFs) are covered in detail in FM 3-90.4/MCWP 3-17.8, *Combined Arms Mobility Operations.*

(1) **Conduct Combined Arms Breaching Operations:** detect, breach or bypass, mark, and proof mined areas and obstacles. Combined arms breaching operations are typically performed in a close combat environment.

(2) **Conduct Clearing Operations:** employ tactics and equipment to detect and eliminate obstacles, mines, and other EHs. While this is not always part of a combined arms breaching operation and is typically not performed in a close combat environment, it will still generally include the task of breach.

(3) **Conduct Gap Crossing Operations:** fill/cross gaps in the terrain/man-made structures to allow personnel and equipment to pass.

(4) **Construct/Maintain Combat Roads and Trails:** expediently prepare or repair routes of travel for personnel and equipment. This includes temporary bypasses of damaged roads and bridges.

(5) **Perform Forward Aviation Combat Engineering:** construct/maintain forward airfields and landing zones (LZs), forward arming and refueling points, landing strips, or other aviation support sites in the forward combat area. This task also includes those actions performed in support of airfield seizure.

b. **Breaching Operations**

(1) Successful breaching operations are characterized by applying the **breaching tenets.** These tenets should be applied whenever an obstacle is encountered in the operational area, whether during an attack or a route clearance operation. These tenets are:

(a) **Intelligence** (includes obstacle intelligence [OBSTINT]).

(b) **Breaching fundamentals** (see Figure III-1).

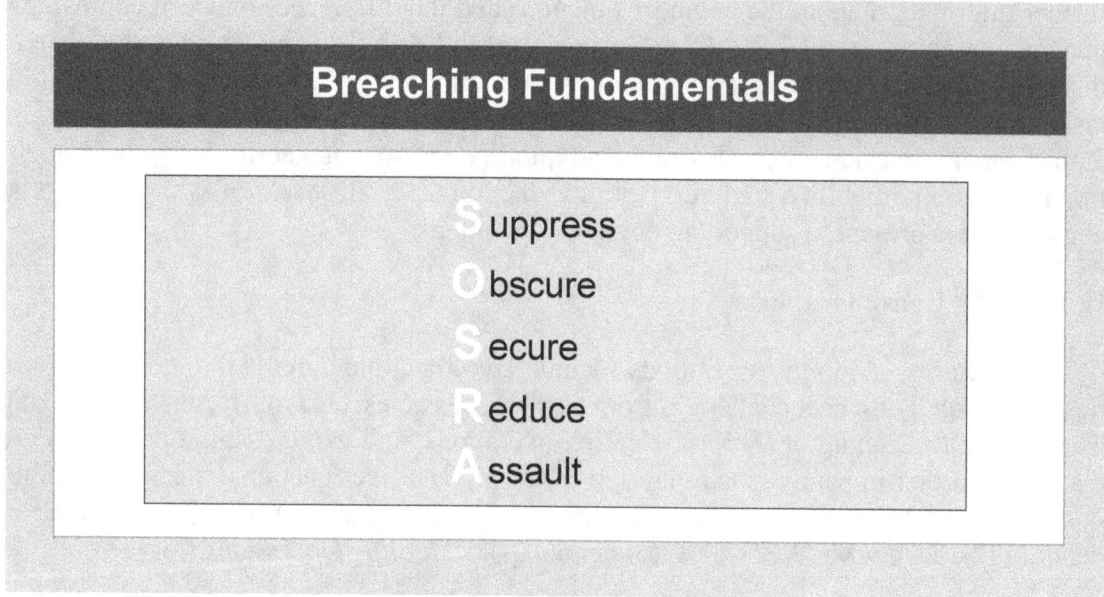

Figure III-1. Breaching Fundamentals

(c) **Breaching organization.**

(d) **Mass.**

(e) **Synchronization.**

(2) Combined arms breaching operations are some of the most complex of modern warfare but are not an end in themselves. They exist only as a part of the maneuver forces' operation that is focused on the objective. The goal of breaching operations is the continued, uninterrupted momentum of ground forces to the objective; therefore, these operations should be planned and executed in support of the ground forces' needs to ensure that actions at the objective are supported by actions at the breach. A **typical sequence** for a breaching consideration is shown in Figure III-2.

(3) As the combined arms team conducts planning for future operations, it may develop a COA requiring breaching operations. Enemy obstacles that disrupt, fix, turn, or block the maneuver force can affect the timing and flow of the operation. Most obstacles will be observed by the enemy and protected with fires; obstacles should be bypassed if possible. For those obstacles that must be breached, constant coordination and integration of all elements of the combined arms team are vital for success. Combat engineers provide significant capability to the combined arms operation and are focused on tactical engineer reconnaissance to include OBSTINT and employing techniques necessary to penetrate obstacles in the path of the force. Geospatial engineering may assist the planning of a deliberate breach. At the brigade combat team (BCT) and the regimental combat team (RCT) level, organic combat engineer companies will typically require augmentation by additional engineer capabilities for most breaching operations. Appendix B, "Land Mobility Capabilities," provides information on those capabilities that are most likely to augment joint forces to conduct mobility operations.

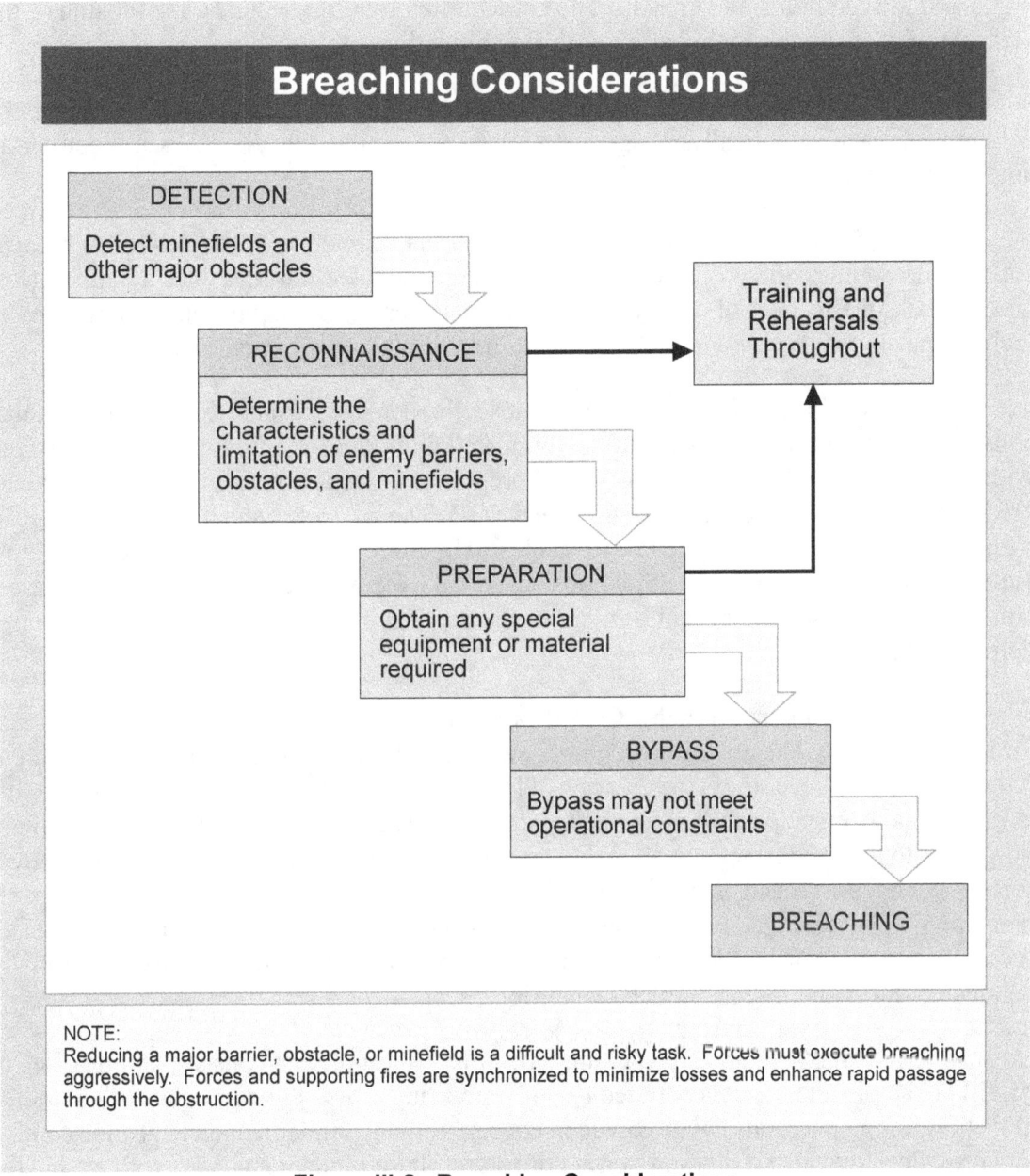

Figure III-2. Breaching Considerations

(4) Breaching operations must be adapted to best exploit the situation. The breaching tenets apply across the continuum of offensive operations, with the level and type of planning distinguishing which of the three general types of breaching operations (deliberate, hasty, and covert) are used to meet the factors of mission, enemy, terrain and weather, troops and support available—time available (METT-T).

(a) **Deliberate Breach.** A deliberate breach is used against a strong defense or complex obstacle system. It is similar to a deliberate attack, requiring detailed knowledge of both the defense and the obstacle systems. It is characterized by prior planning, preparation, and buildup of combat power on the near side of obstacles. Subordinate units are task-organized to accomplish the breach. The breach often requires securing the far side of the obstacle with an assault force before or during reduction.

(b) **Amphibious Breach.** An amphibious breach is an adaptation of the deliberate breach specifically designed to overcome antilanding defenses to conduct an amphibious assault.

(c) **Hasty Breach.** A hasty breach is an adaptation to the deliberate breach-conducted when less time is available. It may be conducted during either a deliberate or hasty attack due to lack of clarity on enemy obstacles or changing enemy situations to include the emplacement of scatterable mines and/or networked munitions.

(d) **In-Stride Breach.** An in-stride breach is a variant of a hasty breach that consists of a rapid breaching adaptation conducted by forces organic to (or task-organized with) the attacking force. It consists of preplanned, well-trained, and well-rehearsed breaching battle drills and the use of the unit's SOP. The in-stride breach takes advantage of surprise and momentum to penetrate obstacles. The force uses the in-stride breach against either weak defenders or very simple obstacles and executes the battle drill on the move. Attacking forces should be configured to execute an in-stride breach except when a deliberate breach is planned.

(e) **Covert Breach.** Covert breaching operations are used to secretly pass through obstacles. The covert breach uses elements of the deliberate and hasty breach as required. Covert breaching is the creation of lanes through minefields or other obstacles that is planned and intended to be executed without detection by an adversary. Its primary purpose is to reduce obstacles in an undetected fashion to facilitate the passage of maneuver forces. A covert breach is conducted when surprise is necessary or desirable. Covert breaching is characterized by using stealth to reduce the obstacles, with support and assault forces executing their mission only if reduction is detected. Covert breaches are normally conducted during periods of reduced visibility.

(5) Combined arms breaching operations require the constant application of METT-T factors and the concentrated use of supporting arms. Fundamentals of combined arms breaching operations have evolved in concert with the fundamentals of ground combat and provide a logical and time-proven set of rules. These fundamentals are reflected in the acronym and memory aid SOSRA as shown in Figure III-1.

(6) The most effective means of countering a mine or other EH is to prevent their employment. Proactive counter operations destroy enemy mine or other EH manufacturing and storage facilities or emplacement capabilities before the mines or EHs are emplaced. Planners must consider enemy storage and mine production facilities and assets for inclusion on the target lists. In addition to destroying mine or EH manufacturing and storage facilities of sites, units must consider targeting enemy engineers and equipment capable of emplacing mines or personnel designated for placing or activating EHs.

c. **Clearing Operations.** Clearing operations are conducted to completely eliminate obstacles, whether along a route or in a specified area. Obstacles may be explosive or nonexplosive. Clearing operations involving explosive obstacles are especially difficult because the detection systems employed are imperfect and available neutralization systems are only partially effective. Clearing operations will not generally be conducted under enemy observation and fire. As with all mobility operations, an intensive reconnaissance effort is imperative to clearing operations. Clearing operations may be conducted in conjunction with or in support of any of the other mobility operations. For example, the establishment of a forward LZ may require an area or route clearance operation to support access to the site.

For additional information about defeating IEDs, see JP 3-15.1, Counter-Improvised Explosive Device Operations.

For a general discussion of clearing (route and area) operations see FM 3-90.4/MCWP 3-17.8, Combined Arms Mobility Operations. *For a discussion of clearing TTP, see FM 3-34.210/MCRP 3-17.2D,* Explosive Hazards Operations; *FM 3-34.214/MCRP 3-17.7L,* Explosives and Demolitions; *and FM 3-90.119/Marine Corps Interim Publication (MCIP) 3-17.01,* Combined Arms Improvised Explosive Device Defeat Operations.

d. **Gap Crossing Operations.** Gap crossing operations are conducted to project combat power over linear obstacles or gaps. There are three general types of gap crossing operations (deliberate, hasty, and covert). The commander, with recommendations from the engineer and other staff members, task-organizes capabilities to support gap crossing operations. At the BCT/RCT level, organic combat engineer companies will typically require augmentation by additional engineer capabilities for most gap crossing operations. Appendix B, "Land Mobility Capabilities," provides information on those capabilities that may be required to augment the BCT/RCT for mobility operations. Combat engineers conduct gap crossings in support of combat maneuver using tactical (assault) bridging equipment to span smaller gaps, heavy equipment (or the employment of fascines and other solutions) to modify the gap, or through the use of expedient bridging (rope bridges, small nonstandard bridging using local materials). Engineers may be tasked to provide additional crossing capabilities such as bridging equipment. River crossing is a unique gap crossing mission that requires specific and dedicated assets from all of the warfighting functions.

For a discussion of river crossing and other types of gap crossings, refer to FM 3-90.12/MCRP 3-17.1, Combined Arms Gap Crossing Operations.

e. **Special Considerations**

(1) The amphibious breach is a type of deliberate breach specifically designed to overcome antilanding defenses in order to conduct an amphibious assault. Units conduct an amphibious breach when no other landing areas are suitable for the landing force (LF). Bypassing an integrated antilanding defense is preferred over conducting an amphibious breach whenever possible; however, the commander must always consider whether a bypass would produce additional risks. Synchronization and teamwork are essential for a successful amphibious breach, which is characterized by thorough reconnaissance, detailed planning, extensive preparation and rehearsal, and a buildup of combat power.

See MCWP 3-17.3, MAGTF Breaching Operations; FM 3-90.4/MCWP 3-17.8, Combined Arms Mobility Operations; NWP 3-15, Naval Mine Warfare; MCRP 3-31.2A/NTTP 3-15.24, Mine Countermeasures in Support of Amphibious Operations; and JP 3-02, Amphibious Operations, for detailed discussions of amphibious breaching operations.

(2) Urban terrain is complex terrain that affects the tactical options available to the commander and requires a thorough knowledge of unique terrain characteristics, detailed planning down to the smallest unit level, and sound leadership at all levels. The complexities of the urban environment, such as line of sight restrictions, inherent fortifications, limited intelligence, densely constructed areas, and the presence of civilians restricts current military technology. US forces do not possess the same overwhelming technological advantages in an urban environment as in other environments.

See FM 3-06.11, Combined Arms Operations in Urban Terrain, and JP 3-06, Joint Urban Operations, for a broader discussion of urban operations.

3. Countermobility Considerations

a. **General.** The objective of barrier, obstacle, and mine warfare employment is to disrupt, fix, turn, or block enemy forces and protect friendly forces. Employment is not an end in itself, but supports the maneuver plan. This section discusses the employment of barriers, obstacles, and scatterable mines/networked munitions employed to counter the enemy's freedom of maneuver. Survivability operations are often integrated with countermobility operations (especially during defensive operations) to support the protection of personnel and equipment overwatching the barriers, obstacles, and minefields as a part of an engagement area.

See FM 90-7, Combined Arms Obstacle Integration, for a more detailed discussion of the employment of barriers, obstacles, and land mines. Also see Appendix C, "Land Countermobility Capabilities."

b. **Terrain Considerations.** Engineers must discern and identify patterns and plan specific detection strategies based on the threat. The proliferation of mines and IEDs requires engineers to continually develop new countering procedures. The integration of explosive ordnance disposal (EOD) capabilities into route or area clearance engineer units has become an increasing requirement.

(1) Engineers play a major role in the JIPOE process by anticipating and providing terrain analysis products of likely contingency areas. Geospatial products assist in describing the environmental effects on enemy and friendly capabilities and broad COAs. Planners use modern automated tools and equipment to create a very detailed analysis of the terrain and weather. The utility and availability of these tools continues to increase, and they provide timely support to time-strapped planners.

(2) Many data management, analysis, and visualization tools are available to assist in the geospatial planning effort. Geospatial engineering provides commanders with terrain analysis and visualization, which improve situational awareness and enhance decision making. Examples of geospatial information useful for planning purposes are as follows:

(a) Three-dimensional terrain fly through capability.

(b) Avenues and routes for joint forces, as well as likely enemy avenues of approach.

(c) Obstacle zone locations.

(d) Potential engagement areas.

(e) Potential unit positions or sites.

(f) Airfield and port information and capabilities.

(g) Support to urban operations and other complex terrain.

(h) High-payoff target information.

(i) Deep-target information.

(j) Communications or visual line of sight.

(k) Locations of LOCs and main supply routes and potential locations of base camps.

(l) Identification of flood plains and potential LZs.

(m) Fused data from multiple databases.

(3) Terrain analysis is a key product of geospatial support. It is the study of the terrain's properties and how they change over time, with use, and under varying weather conditions. Terrain analysis starts with the collection, verification, processing, revision, and construction of source data. It requires the analysis of climatology (current and forecasted weather conditions), soil conditions, and enemy or friendly vehicle performance metrics. Terrain analysis and geospatial information and services (GI&S) are necessary to support mission planning and operational requirements. GI&S requires the management of an enterprise geospatial database at every echelon from combatant command to deployed maneuver forces. Terrain analysis is a technical process and requires the expertise of geospatial information technicians and a geospatial engineer.

(4) Geospatial engineering is generating, managing, analyzing, and disseminating positionally accurate terrain information that is tied to some portion of the earth's surface. These actions provide mission-tailored data, tactical decision aids, and visualization products that define the character of the zone for the maneuver commander. Key aspects of the geospatial engineering mission are databases, analysis, digital products, visualization, and printed maps. Both organic and augmenting geospatial engineer capabilities at the theater, corps, division, and brigade levels are responsible for geospatial engineering.

(5) The characterization of effective geospatial engineering lies in this ability to effectively go outside the engineer community and work with other staff sections, organizations, and agencies. As such, coordination across functional areas focused on supporting various missions becomes critical. This coordination contains, but is not limited to, the ability to fully define requirements; discover and obtain the geospatial data; put it into a usable form; and then use, share, and maintain with those mission partners. It is the geospatial engineer who, through this process, enables the commander and staff to leverage geospatial information to the fullest extent possible.

(6) Geospatial information that is timely, accurate, and relevant is a critical enabler for the operations process. Geospatial engineers assist in the analysis of the meaning of activities and significantly contribute to anticipating, estimating, and warning of possible future events. Geospatial information provides the foundation for developing shared situational awareness and improving understanding of our forces, our capabilities, the adversary, and other conditions of the operational environment. Geospatial regional analysis product examples include the following:

(a) Statistical analysis—IED and insurgent networks.

(b) Significant activities database analysis to determine tactics and emerging trends.

(c) Capabilities and readiness of enemy forces.

(d) Climatic impacts on operations.

(e) Route analysis.

(f) Sectarian demographics.

(g) Nonstandard or mission-specific geospatial products.

(7) Geospatial functional analysis sample products graphically describe the following:

(a) Industries and energy.

(b) Telecommunications infrastructure.

(c) Underground facilities and caves.

(d) Political boundaries.

(8) The geospatial engineer uses analysis and visualization capabilities to integrate people, processes, and tools using multiple information sources and collaborative analysis to build a shared knowledge of the physical environment. Whether it is using one of the examples indicated above, or through some other special product, the geospatial engineer, in

combination with other engineers and staff officers, provides support to the unit's mission and commander's intent.

(9) Geospatial engineering is provided to joint forces based on echelon. It is focused on data generation, data management, and quality control at the combatant command level. At the corps and division levels, the majority of the workload is required to support database management, mission planning, and the JIPOE process. Below division level, geospatial engineering is increasingly focused on current operations and updating the geospatial database (database management).

(10) The geospatial engineering units available to the commander may become part of the command's GEOINT cell. The GEOINT cell is comprised of the people and capabilities that constitute the GEOINT support, to include the imagery and geospatial assets. The cell ensures that GEOINT requirements are coordinated through appropriate channels as applicable and facilitates shared access.

(11) This cell may be centrally located or distributed throughout the command and connected by networks. Cell members do not have to work directly for a designated GEOINT officer; they may still work for their parent unit, but coordinate efforts across staff directorates. The key to a successful process is collaboration across the functional areas within the command and between the GEOINT cell, higher headquarters, and the rest of the stakeholders.

c. **Employment Principles**

(1) Barriers, obstacles, and minefields should be evaluated from both an offensive and a defensive posture.

(2) Barriers, obstacles, and minefields should directly support the maneuver plan.

(3) Reinforcing obstacles should be integrated with existing barriers and obstacles to support the commander's intent and operational concept.

(4) Barriers, obstacles, and minefields are more effective when employed in depth.

(5) By varying the type, design, and location of reinforcing obstacles, the enemy's breaching operation is made more difficult.

(6) The effectiveness of barrier, obstacle, and mine employment can be affected by the air situation.

(7) Coverage by observation and by direct or indirect fire is essential to restrict enemy breaching efforts, maneuver, and massing of forces and to increase the destruction of enemy forces. Planned on-call fires (indirect and/or direct) are ideal for this purpose.

d. **Countermobility Resources.** The employment of scatterable mines/networked munitions and other obstacles to support the friendly scheme of maneuver is resource-intensive. Combat engineers and others must have the barrier materials, mines, demolitions, and wire as well as the equipment needed to emplace/build the obstacles. There will often be competing priorities for the use of engineers and the materials and equipment needed to perform the work to support the obstacle effort. The following four categories provide a useful framework for identifying the resources required for effective countermobility operations:

(1) **Land mines are categorized as either persistent or nonpersistent.** Both categories provide anti-vehicle and AP capabilities. **Persistent mines are no longer authorized for use by US forces (except as noted in Chapter 1, "Introduction," paragraph 4.b, "US Law and Policy").** Many persistent mines are activated by pressure or contact. These mines are emplaced by hand or mechanical means, buried or surface emplaced, and normally emplaced in a pattern that aids recording. Mechanical emplacement may be restricted by terrain conditions. The emplacement of persistent minefields is normally time-, manpower-, and logistics-intensive. **Scatterable mines are most commonly used by technically advanced nations and are emplaced without regard to classical patterns.** Although locations of each individual mine cannot be precisely recorded, scatterable minefields can be accurately recorded to within 10 meters when emplaced. They are emplaced by ground mine dispensing systems, artillery, aircraft, or by hand. They are designed to self-destruct after a set period of time, ranging from four hours to 15 days. Scatterable mines significantly reduce manpower requirements associated with MW. Smaller and lighter, these mines reduce logistics requirements because of their reduced bulk and weight. Scatterable mines also make it possible to emplace minefields quickly and, importantly, to do so deep in the enemy's rear area such as at an air base, LOCs, air defense site, or an assembly area. Aircraft and artillery are the most flexible and responsive means of scatterable mine delivery; however, they often have other competing roles. Other disadvantages include time and high number of artillery rounds or aircraft sorties required to emplace a minefield. These factors increase the exposure of emplacing artillery to counter battery fires and emplacing aircraft or helicopters to enemy air defenses. Networked munitions are a class of remotely controlled, interconnected weapons systems that can be rapidly emplaced, consisting of nonpersistent (self-destructing/self-deactivating) AVL/APL munitions that provide ground-based countermobility and protection capabilities through persistent surveillance and the scalable application of lethal and nonlethal means (see Figure III-3).

> **An example of networked munitions is the newly fielded Spider system. This system is interoperable with the Army Battle Command by utilizing data feed sets to populate a common operating picture. This system provides man-in-the-loop operations and on-off-on capability, permitting the passage of friendly forces on demand and reducing incidents of fratricide and unintended engagements on civilians.**

(2) **Demolition obstacles are created by the detonation of explosives.** Demolition is generally used to create tactical level obstacles. However, it can also be used to create operational obstacles such as the destruction of major dams, bridges, and railways, as well as highways through built-up areas or terrain choke points. Demolition obstacles are

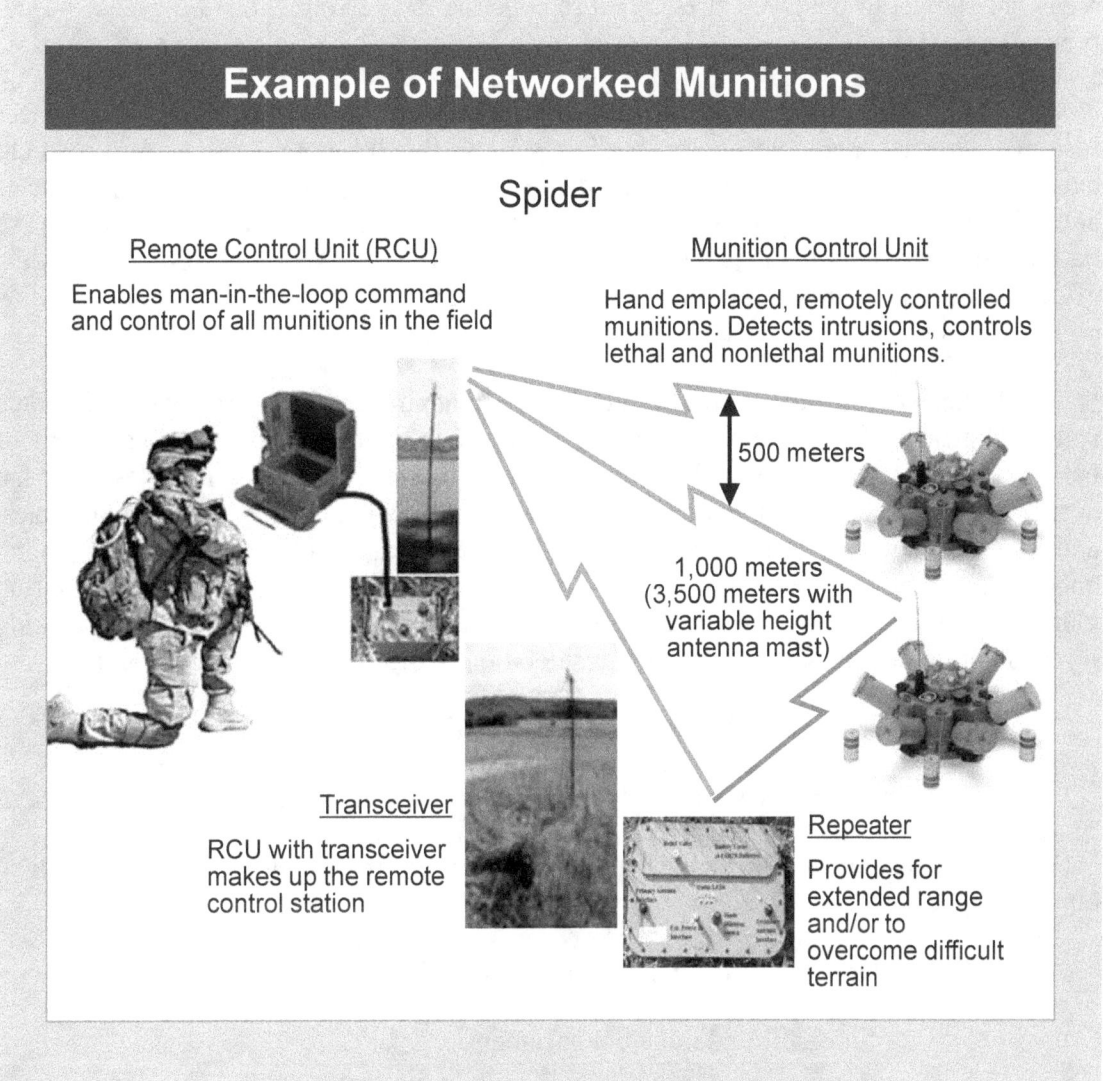

Figure III-3. Example of Networked Munitions

typically classified as preliminary or reserved obstacles. **Preliminary obstacles are those planned by subordinate commanders,** are not considered critical to the JFC's plan, and can be detonated as soon as they are prepared or as the situation dictates. **Reserved obstacles are those deemed critical to the JFC's or subordinate commander's plan and are detonated only when directed by the commander who designated them.** Demolition obstacles may require lengthy completion time and large quantities of demolition materials because of the size and characteristics of the target.

(3) **Constructed obstacles are man-made,** created without the use of explosives. Typical tactical examples are barbed wire obstacles and anti-vehicle ditches. Operational and strategic barriers and obstacles may also be constructed. Examples are fortified areas and lines. These large-scale obstructions generally require extensive time, manpower, equipment, and material. In general, engineers will play a major role in obstacles of this magnitude. Constructed barriers and obstacles should be emplaced before hostilities or in

areas not subject to observed fires, because construction personnel can be exposed to all types of enemy fire.

(4) **Field expedient obstacles.** When mines, barrier materials, or engineer resources are not available or are in short supply, the JFC may have to rely on field expedients such as abatis, flame field expedient, or IED for employment in place of obstacles and minefields. Field expedients can be hastily constructed from materials found on the battlefield, such as containers, fuel, and explosive devices. They can provide a quick, effective means for providing a limited offensive and defensive obstacle capability when conventional resources are not available.

e. **Offensive Employment.** During offensive planning, the JFC, through the joint force staff, identifies priority locations and plans and coordinates the joint emplacement of barriers, obstacles, and minefields. Under some circumstances, the JFC may designate the systems that subordinate commanders utilize for emplacement. These barriers, obstacles, and minefields generally focus on isolating the battlefield, facilitating economy of force, enhancing overall force security, and blocking or disrupting an enemy's withdrawal. During planning and deployment, care must be taken to ensure that the mobility of the attacking force is not hindered. Key factors for consideration in offensive employment are:

(1) The scheme of maneuver for the operation.

(2) Current enemy situation capabilities, intent, and probable COAs.

(3) Accurate terrain analysis to determine where friendly forces are vulnerable to counterattack.

(4) Preplanning, deconfliction, and coordination with other components.

(5) C2 of obstacle and mine emplacement.

(6) Information flow to inform friendly forces of friendly and enemy barrier, obstacle, and minefield locations using the standard report formats.

f. **Defensive Employment.** During defensive planning, the JFC, through the joint force staff, identifies priority locations and plans and coordinates the joint emplacement of barriers, obstacles, and minefields. Under some circumstances, the JFC may designate the systems that subordinate commanders use for emplacement. The primary intent of defensive barrier, obstacle, and mine warfare employment is to degrade enemy capabilities by disrupting combat formations and their movement, interfering with C2, and confusing enemy commanders. The secondary intent is to destroy or attrit enemy forces. Key factors for consideration in defensive employment are as follows:

(1) Current enemy situation, capabilities, intent, and probable COAs.

(2) Confirmation of where the maneuver commander has designated engagement areas and intends to engage the enemy.

Logistics planning must provide for replacement of special equipment and materials to support breaching operations.

(3) Confirmation of the scheme of maneuver for the defense.

(4) Accurate terrain analysis to determine where friendly forces are vulnerable to enemy attack.

(5) Preplanning, deconfliction, and coordination with other components.

(6) C2 of obstacle and mine emplacement.

(7) Information flow to inform friendly forces of friendly and enemy barrier, obstacle, and minefield locations using the standard report formats.

(8) Integration of barrier, obstacle, and minefield emplacement complements the plan for defense.

(9) Emplacement of nonpersistent minefields and other time- or labor-intensive obstacles before the beginning of hostilities in order to reduce the exposure to enemy fire.

(10) Preplanned employment of scatterable minefields throughout the operational environment. The choice of scatterable systems is mission-dependent. Ground emplaced mine scattering systems are best for rapidly emplacing large minefields in friendly controlled areas. Artillery or aircraft-delivered systems are employed throughout the battlefield. The appropriateness of artillery or aircraft delivery systems varies depending on the threat conditions and other mission priorities; however, organic systems should be employed whenever possible.

(11)   The timetable for friendly operations may be upset or cause fratricide if the wrong self-destruct settings are used. Emplacement of nonpersistent scatterable minefields is not nearly as labor-intensive as the old conventional munitions, but the planning has to be precise for their placement and the time duration set on the munitions for the self-destruct time of four hours, 48 hours, or 15 days.

(12) Obscurants, used as a limited obstacle to canalize or slow advancing enemy forces. When combined with barriers, obstacles, and/or minefields, obscurants can enhance the vulnerability of enemy forces by limiting their visual, target-acquisition, and intelligence-gathering capabilities.

g. **Other Considerations.**   The overriding consideration in planning obstacles is accomplishment of the mission; however, there are three considerations that are key to the military mission.

(1) **Legal Restrictions.** The creation and employment of countermobility barriers, obstacles, and mines must comply with the law of war, international law, and US law and policy. The JFC will ensure that the staff judge advocate is integrated throughout the planning process and that countermobility plans—especially those involving the emplacement of mines—receive a final legal review prior to execution.

(2) **Obstacle-Clearing Operations at the Cessation of Hostilities.** Obstacle-clearing operations continued for years in Kuwait following the end of the 1990–1991 Persian Gulf War, largely due to a lack of accurate minefield records by the defending Iraqi forces. Mine and minefields continued to threaten civilians long after hostilities were concluded and caused numerous casualties to military and civilian personnel. Accurate reporting, recording, and tracking not only will prevent fratricide but will expedite clearing operations when peace is restored.

For a general discussion of clearing (route and area) operations see FM 3-90.4/MCWP 3-17.8, Combined Arms Mobility Operations. *For a discussion of clearing TTP, see FM 3-34.210/MCRP 3-17.2D,* Explosive Hazards Operations; *FM 3-34.214/MCRP 3-17.7L,* Explosives and Demolitions; *and FM 3-90.119/MCIP 3-17.01,* Combined Arms Improvised Explosive Device Defeat Operations. *See also Appendix F, "Humanitarian Mine Action," for more discussion.*

(3) **Impacts of Obstacles on Civilians and Their Environment.** Obstacles frequently modify terrain through demolition, excavation, and other means. Some obstacle actions, such as destroying levees, setting fires, felling trees in forested areas, or demolishing bridges, may have immediate impacts on civilians and often will have long-term effects on them and the environment and are governed by the law of armed conflict. Commanders must minimize the impact of obstacles on civilians and the environment if militarily possible. For example, if the enemy can be prevented from using a bridge by means other than demolishing it, commanders may choose the less damaging COA. Efforts should be undertaken to mark minefields to prevent harm to civilians. Commanders must avoid unnecessary destruction of farmland or forests or pollution of water sources when creating obstacles. Care exercised by commanders will alleviate long-term negative effects on

civilians, friendly forces, and the environment. Moreover, application of the principles of proportionality and military necessity are legal requirements under the law of armed conflict.

4. Command and Control

a. **Planning.** Commanders and staffs consider both friendly and enemy use of obstacles when planning operations. At the tactical level, assured mobility planning brings focus to mobility, countermobility, and survivability task planning in support of breaching, clearing, and gap crossing operations. At the tactical level, commanders focus on identifying the scheme of maneuver that must be supported by mobility and/or countermobility efforts. At the operational level, countermobility planning focuses on granting obstacle emplacement authority or providing obstacle control. At each level, commanders include obstacle planning in the decision-making process. This ensures that a combined arms approach to mobility operations, as well as countermobility obstacle integration, is effective in support of the maneuver plan.

b. **Reconnaissance.** Reconnaissance is performed before, during, and after mobility operations to provide information used in the planning process as well as by the commander to formulate, confirm, or modify the COA. The information gathered through reconnaissance, other geospatial products, and terrain analysis supports the mobility operation. Tactical reconnaissance supporting mobility operations should focus on OBSTINT—those collection efforts conducted to detect the presence of enemy (and natural) obstacles, determine their types and dimensions, and provide the necessary information to plan appropriate combined arms breaching, clearance, or bypass operations to negate the impact on the friendly scheme of maneuver. Tactical reconnaissance also allows friendly forces to anticipate when and where the enemy may employ obstacles that could impede operations as well as verify the condition of natural or other man-made obstacles.

c. **Control Means.** The purpose of obstacle control is to synchronize subordinate obstacle efforts with the commander's intent and scheme of maneuver. Commanders exercise obstacle control by granting or withholding obstacle emplacement authority or restricting obstacles through orders or other specific guidance. However, commanders must be cognizant that lack of obstacle control measures may result in obstacles that interfere with the higher commander's scheme of maneuver, while excessive obstacle control may result in a lack of obstacles that support the refined fire plans of subordinate commanders. Commanders and staffs consider width, depth, and time when they conduct obstacle-control planning. The following considerations guide this planning:

(1) **Support current operations.**

(2) **Maximize subordinate flexibility.**

(3) **Facilitate future operations.**

d. **Reporting, Recording, and Marking**

(1) Intelligence concerning enemy minefields is reported by the fastest means available. Spot reports (SPOTREPs) are the tactical commander's most common source of

minefield intelligence. They originate from patrols that have been sent on specific minefield reconnaissance missions or from units that have discovered mine information in the course of their normal operations. The information is transmitted to higher headquarters and tracked in joint minefield and obstacle databases.

(2) Lane or bypass marking is a critical component of obstacle reduction. Effective lane marking allows commanders to project forces through an obstacle quickly, with combat power and C2 intact. It gives an assault force and follow-on forces confidence in the safety of the lane and helps prevent unnecessary casualties.

FM 3-90.4/MCWP 3-17.8, Combined Arms Mobility Operations, *and MCWP 3-17.3,* MAGTF Breaching Operations, *provide detailed discussions of marking operations.*

CHAPTER IV
MARITIME OPERATIONS

"The clever combatant imposes his will on the enemy, but does not allow the enemy's will to be imposed on him."

Sun Tzu, *The Art of War*

1. General Discussion

a. **General.** Maritime MW consists of the strategic, operational, and tactical employment of sea mines and mine countermeasures (MCM). MW is divided into two categories: the emplacement of mines to degrade the enemy's capabilities to wage land, air, and maritime warfare; and the countering of enemy mining capability or emplaced mines in order to permit friendly maneuver. Naval MW has played a significant role in every major armed conflict involving the United States since the Revolutionary War. Mines can be inexpensive, easy to procure, reliable, effective, and difficult for intelligence agencies to track. More than 50 of the world's navies have mine emplacing capability while a considerable number of countries, many of which are known mine exporters, actively engage in development and manufacture of new models. Although many of these stockpiled mines are relatively old, they remain lethal and can often be upgraded.

b. As adversaries have pursued irregular means they have introduced the IED threat to the maritime domain. Boats laden with explosives or WBIEDs can be used against ships and areas connected to water. An early example of this type was the Japanese Shinyo suicide boats during World War II. These explosive-laden boats were successful in damaging or sinking several American ships. More recently, suicide bombers used a WBIED to attack the USS COLE in the port of Aden. In Iraq, US and United Kingdom troops have been killed by WBIEDs. The next few years are likely to bring maritime conflict and WBIEDs into sharp focus as the proliferation of IED knowledge spreads in extremist networks. A further use of minefields by adversaries is to accentuate the effectiveness of other weapons and thereby provide a suitable environment for their use rather than a primary weapon. This may be achieved by using minefields to channel shipping into selected killing areas or restrict their maneuverability.

c. Naval MW employs a broad campaign approach, incorporating offensive and defensive aspects of MW throughout the range of military operations. To achieve national and military objectives in the short term, mining campaigns may be defeated without necessarily having to destroy the minefields. If US forces can prevent mines from being employed, avoid the minefield, or force the enemy to deploy a tactically insignificant minefield, then objectives can be achieved.

d. **Legal Considerations in the Employment of Mines.** The use of naval mines is governed by Hague Convention VII of 1907, which limits the type, method of use, and tactics used by nations employing mines. Other international agreements, as well as US and allied peacetime ROE and ROE during armed conflict, constrain the commander contemplating their use. All joint commanders involved in MW, whether mining, MCM, or both, should be familiar with these legal considerations. A more detailed discussion of international law relative to naval mines is contained in NWP 3-15, *Naval Mine Warfare*.

2. Mine Warfare Command and Control

a. **JFC.** Naval MW is an enabler of joint force operations. The JFC is supported in MW by the Navy component commander (NCC), or if assigned, a combined or joint force maritime component commander (JFMCC).

b. **NCC or JFMCC.** The NCC or JFMCC staff supports the JFC with all operational-level military operations at sea, including MW. As such, the NCC staff should integrate MW into their planning. The Naval Mine and Anti-Submarine Warfare Command (NMAWC) maintains a deployable staff to provide phased, scalable MW expertise and support to NCCs.

c. **Mine Warfare Commander (MIWC).** The MIWC is a supporting warfare commander to the NCC or the officer in tactical command and is the commander's primary advisor on all aspects of MW—both mining and MCM. NMAWC can serve as the MIWC and perform the MW functions in support of the NCC.

d. **MCM Commander (MCMC).** The MCMC is the supporting commander to the MIWC or designated commander for MCM within an assigned area. Depending on the extent of operations and geography, it is conceivable to have multiple MCMCs under the coordination of a single MIWC. United States Navy (USN) MCM squadrons (MCMRONs) exist to fulfill the MCMC role, and are the preferred choice for MCM planning and force C2. The MCMC controls the operations of MCM assets (surface MCM [SMCM] vessels, airborne MCM [AMCM] squadrons/detachments, and underwater MCM [UMCM] elements) in the operational area.

3. Environmental Considerations

a. Environmental considerations are significant in MW and affect both mining and MCM. Mine cases, mine sensors, target signals, and MCM systems are all impacted by environmental factors and impact the selection of equipment and procedures.

b. **Influence of the Environment.** In strategic, operational, and tactical planning for both mining and MCM, the environment must be considered. Mining success depends largely on the suitability of the environment for both weapons delivery and effectiveness after mine placement. Environmental factors that should be considered when deciding to conduct exploratory and reconnaissance operations, as well as employment techniques, are provided in Figure IV-1.

ENVIRONMENTAL CONSIDERATIONS IN MINE WARFARE		
Category	**Factors**	**Major Operation Impact**
Coastal topography and landmarks	Marginal topography, natural and man-made landmarks, aircraft flight path hazards, shoals, and other underwater hazards to surface craft	Navigational control, accuracy flight restrictions, and pattern controls
Atmospheric characteristics	Climatic conditions, duration of darkness and light, visibility, air temperature, winds, precipitation, storm frequency, and icing conditions	All operational limitations and restrictions common to adverse atmospheric conditions, platform and equipment selection, force level requirements, and logistic concerns
Water depth	Bathymetry, seasonal storms, river run-off	Extent of operational area in relation to mine type to be countered, choice of countermeasures, platforms, gear and tactics; limits to diver employment
Sea and surf	Sea and swell condition, surf characteristics	Operational limits for surface craft, explosive ordnance disposal personnel, and mine countermeasures equipment; actuation probability for pressure mines; rate and direction of sweep or hunt; mine detection capability
Currents	Surface and subsurface current patterns, including tidal, surf, and riverine-originated currents	Navigation and maneuver of displacement craft and towed equipment; navigational error; diver operation limitations; effect on mine burial
Ice conditions	Thickness and extent of sea ice	Modify, restrict, or preclude operations depending on extent and thickness of ice
Water column properties	Water temperature, salinity, and clarity	Temperature effects on diver operations; ability to visually or optically locate moored or bottom mines; temperature/salinity compilation of conductivity for magnetic sweep; sonar depth and effectiveness
Seabed characteristics	Bottom roughness, material, strength, and stability	Decision to employ minehunting techniques; limitations on mechanical sweep gear; extent to which a mine will bury
Acoustic environment	Sound velocity profile, acoustic propagation/attenuation, acoustic scattering, and reverberation	Sonar settings, ranges, and effectiveness, acoustic sweep path and sweep safety, number of minelike contacts, and sonar hunting efficiency
Magnetic environment	Electrical conductivity, number of magnetic minelike contacts, ambient magnetic background	Ability to employ open electrode sweeps; extent and strength of magnetic field established by magnetic sweep gear; number of minelike targets limiting magnetic hunt efficiency; effectiveness of magnetometer detectors
Pressure environment	Natural pressure fluctuations due to wave action	Actuation probability for pressure mines and, hence, the selection of conventional or guinea pig sweep techniques
Biologic environment	Bio-fouling conditions, hazardous marine life	Ability to detect and classify mines visually or with sonar; marine life presenting potential hazard to divers

Figure IV-1. Environmental Considerations in Mine Warfare

4. Elements of Mine Warfare

MW can be applied across the range of military operations and can be divided into the subdisciplines of mining and MCM. These are further divided into various areas, depicted in Figure IV-2, and discussed below.

5. Mining

Mining is used to support the broad tasks of establishing and maintaining control of essential sea areas. Mining embraces all methods whereby naval mines are used to deny sea area or inflict damage on adversary shipping to hinder, disrupt, and deny adversary operations.

a. **Mining Objectives.** In MW, mining has application in all phases of joint operations. US mining can be employed to reduce the adversary's threat to friendly forces and preserve access. Mining complements and comprises an essential part of other warfare areas, particularly strike, antisubmarine, and antisurface warfare. Sea mines, or the implicit threat of their possible presence, may deny the enemy use of sea areas vital to their operations.

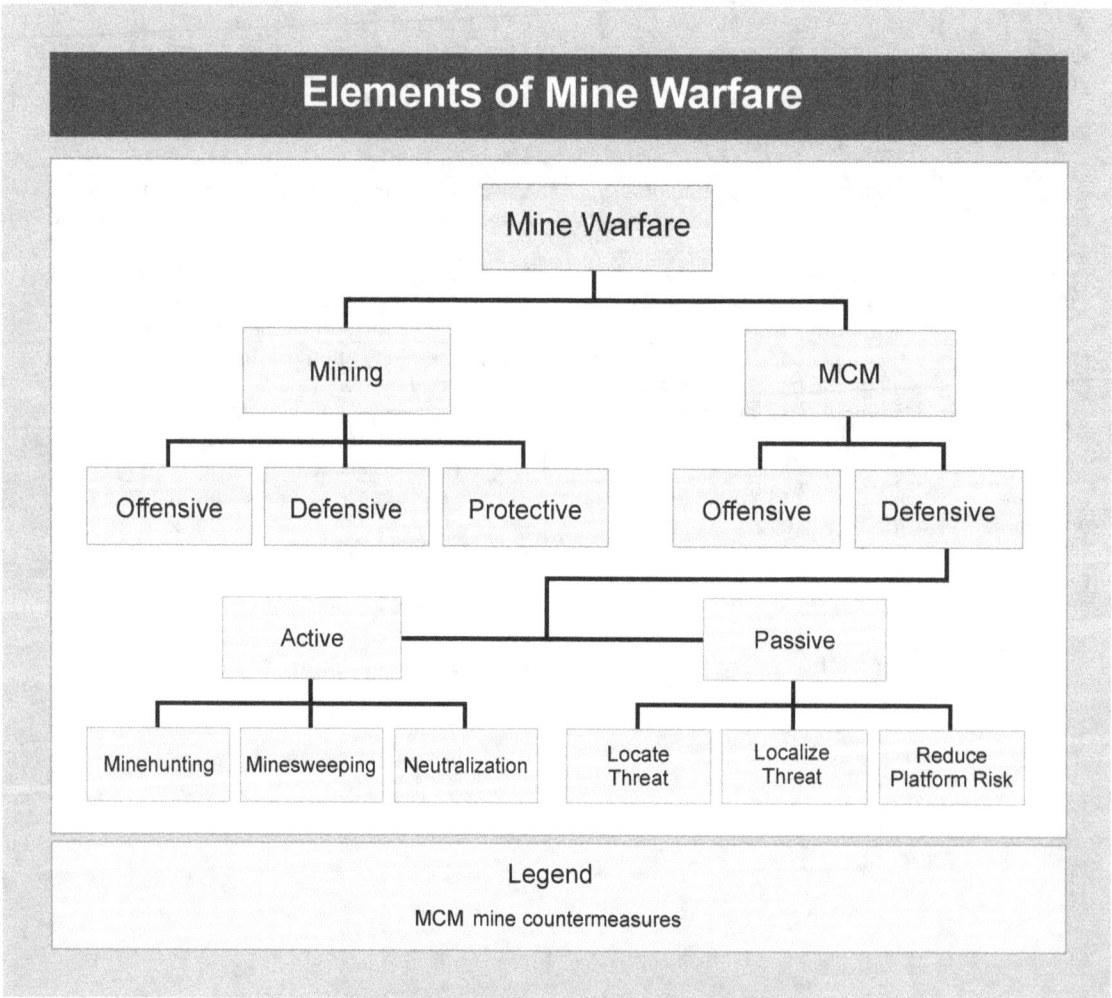

Figure IV-2. Elements of Mine Warfare

Conversely, mines may be used to protect friendly harbors, channels, and shores. Delays and interruptions in the shipping of war-sustaining materiel may deprive the enemy of critical offensive and defensive capabilities. Enemy ships confined to their bases or deterred in transit by mining operations become ineffective in their contribution to the war effort, and delays in shipping may be as costly as actual losses.

b. **US Mining Policy.** In the event of war, US policy will be to conduct offensive, defensive, and protective mining as necessary. The decision to employ mines is typically made by the CCDR or higher authority, depending on ROE. The purpose is to reduce the enemy threat by destruction and disruption of their operations, to interdict the enemy SLOCs and designated ports in order to neutralize or destroy combatant and merchant ships, and to defend US and allied shipping. More specifically, naval mines may be used in conjunction with other warfare forces to aid in sea control by:

(1) Deterring enemy use of naval mines.

(2) Denying enemy use of designated ocean areas, ports, or waterways for diplomatic, economic, or military purposes.

(3) Influencing enemy maneuver and direction or otherwise restricting the enemy's movements to buttress the operational effectiveness of friendly forces.

MK-65 Quickstrike mine being attached to airframe.

(4) Protecting ports, coastal lines of passage, opening preplanned shipping lanes (Q-routes), and designated operating areas.

(5) Destroying enemy ships and submarines directly.

(6) Establishing blockades to provide political leverage in a limited war situation.

(7) Denying the enemy the ability to carry out amphibious operations, or in support of friendly amphibious operations.

c. **Mining Assets.** Mining is generally conducted by United States Air Force (USAF) or USN strike aircraft. Submarines and surface ships can also be configured for mine emplacement operations. Given the joint warfare aspects of mining, the NCC's MW staff must work in coordination with the strike and target planning staffs.

For additional information on maritime mining capabilities, refer to Appendix D, "Maritime Mining Capabilities," and NTTP 3-15.1, Maritime Mining.

6. Mine Countermeasures

MCM is the second area of MW. MCM includes all actions undertaken to prevent enemy mines from altering friendly forces' maritime plans, operations, or maneuver. MCM reduces the threat of mines and the effects of enemy-emplaced sea mines on friendly naval force and seaborne logistics force access to and transit of selected waterways.

a. MCM operations are divided into two broad areas: offensive and defensive MCM (see Figure IV-3).

(1) **Offensive MCM.** The most effective means of countering a mine threat is to prevent the emplacement of mines. Offensive MCM involves deterring or destroying enemy mining capability before the mines are emplaced. Although essential to offensive MCM, these operations are not normally conducted by naval MW forces. MW planners must ensure that enemy mine emplacer, mine storage and, ultimately, mine production facilities and assets are considered for inclusion on joint target lists.

(2) **Defensive MCM.** Defensive countermeasures are designed to counter mines once they have been emplaced. MCM can be conducted following the termination of conflict solely to eliminate or reduce the threat to shipping posed by residual sea mines. However, most defensive MCM operations are undertaken during conflict to support (enable) other maritime operations, such as sea control or power projection. Defensive MCM includes passive and active MCM.

(a) Passive MCM reduces the threat from emplaced mines without physically attacking the mine itself, through reduction of ship susceptibility to mine actuation. Three primary passive measures are practiced: localization of the threat, detection and avoidance of the minefield, and risk reduction.

Maritime Mine Countermeasures

Offensive

Prevent the emplacement of mines through...
- destroying enemy mine manufacturing facilities
- destroying enemy mine storage facilities
- destroying enemy mine emplacing platforms

Defensive

Counter mines once they have been emplaced through...
Passive mine countermeasuares
- localization of threat utilizing Q-routes
- detection and avoidance of minefields
- risk reduction
Active mine countermeasures
- minehunting
- minesweeping

Figure IV-3. Maritime Mine Countermeasures

1. Localization of the threat is aided by the establishment of a system of transit routes for friendly forces. These routes may be designated as Q-routes, to be used by friendly shipping to minimize exposure in potentially mined waters. Establishment of transit routes should be one of the first steps taken by MCM planners, if routes have not been designated previously.

2. Detection and avoidance of minefields can be accomplished by exploiting intelligence information or by MCM efforts. When mine location has been established, shipping may be routed around the area.

3. Risk reduction consists primarily of ship self-protection measures rather than MCM force activity. Risk may be reduced by controlling the degree of potential interaction with a mine sensor. Against contact mines, a reduction in draft and posting additional lookouts can reduce the number of mines the ship's hull might strike. Influence mines can be denied the required activation signals by controlling the ship's emissions. Use of on-board magnetic field reduction equipment or external degaussing, silencing a ship to minimize radiated noise, or using minimum speeds to reduce pressure signature are examples of operational risk reduction. Other types of risk reduction involve the enhancement of ship survivability in the event of mine detonation.

*USS DEVASTATOR, avenger class
mine countermeasure vessel.*

(b) Active MCM is employed when passive countermeasures alone cannot protect shipping traffic. This entails physical interference with the explosive function of the mine or actually destroying it. Minehunting and minesweeping are the primary techniques employed in active MCM. Both require detailed intelligence and planning by the MCMC to counter the threat.

<u>1.</u> **Minehunting.** Minehunting is the employment of sensor and neutralization systems, whether air, surface, or subsurface, to locate and dispose of individual mines. Minehunting is conducted to eliminate mines in a known field when sweeping is not feasible or desirable, or to verify the presence or absence of mines in a given area. When mines are located, mine neutralization is performed through the use of systems such as remote-controlled vehicles, EOD divers, or marine mammal systems. Minehunting poses less risk to MCM forces, covers an area more thoroughly, and provides a higher probability of mine detection than minesweeping.

<u>2.</u> **Minesweeping.** Minesweeping is conducted by either surface craft or aircraft and involves the towing of mechanical or influence sweep systems. Mechanical sweeping employs specially equipped cables to sever moored mine cables so that the mines

float to the surface, where they can be destroyed by EOD divers. Influence sweeping involves the use of towed or streamed devices that emit signals emulating target ships to trigger influence mines.

b. **Intelligence Support**

(1) **Intelligence Gathering.** Prior to MW operations, intelligence may indicate the types, quantities, or locations of mine storage sites. This information can cue the surveillance of mine storage sites to detect the movement of mines. Intelligence of mine movement to mine emplacing platforms and the subsequent movement of the mine emplacing platforms can provide advance information to ascertain the type, size, and location of minefields. Where mining is a possible threat, tracking and intelligence collection should begin early and be sufficiently systematic to provide confident estimates of mine activity.

(2) **Mine Exploitation.** A key element of mine countermeasure is detailed knowledge of the mine sensor and targeting circuitry. Intelligence on enemy mine emplacement operations can aid in determining the type of sensor and style of target processing used. Accurate data can be acquired by actually exploiting a mine recovered during MCM operations. Exploitation may provide information on mine settings and mine modification intelligence.

Minesweeping is a method of active maritime countermeasure and is conducted by either surface craft or aircraft.

c. **Planning Considerations.** The MCM planning process starts with an estimate of the situation and a mission statement that results in production of an MCM tasking order. Some aspects of the mission definition must be provided by the supporting commander.

(1) **Objectives.** The mission statement includes an objective for active MCM, an acceptable risk factor, and a specific operational area. The MCMC shall choose a specific objective from the list in Figure IV-4, as described below.

(a) **Exploratory.** The objective of exploration is to determine whether or not mines are present and is usually the first objective when an enemy minefield is suspected.

(b) **Reconnaissance.** Reconnaissance operations are designed to make a rapid assessment of the limits of a mined area and the estimated number and types of mines present.

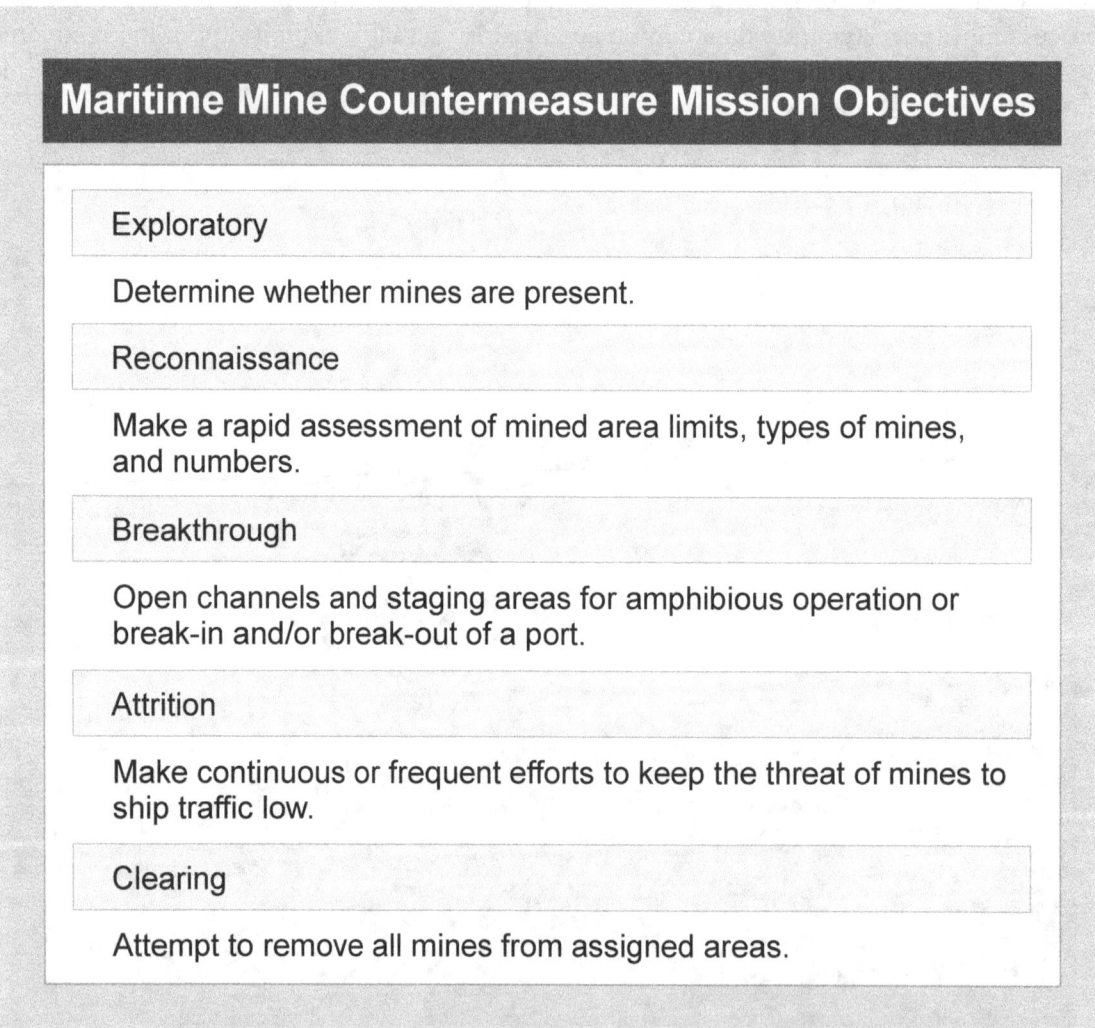

Figure IV-4. Maritime Mine Countermeasure Mission Objectives

(c) **Breakthrough.** The breakthrough objective is directed when rapidity is required to open channels and staging areas for an amphibious operation or port break-in and/or break-out. The goal is to reduce the threat to friendly shipping passing through the mine threat area in the specified time available for MCM.

(d) **Attrition.** Attrition objectives call for continuous or frequent MCM efforts to keep the threat of mines to ship traffic as low as possible when traffic must continue to transit the mined waters for a comparatively long period of time.

(e) **Clearing.** The objective of clearing is to remove the greatest number of mines from the assigned area, thus reducing risk to friendly shipping to a specified acceptable risk.

(2) **Risk Directives.** MCM techniques are inherently hazardous when used against certain mine types. To determine the proper MCM technique to employ, the MCMC must, in addition to an objective, be given direction regarding the maximum acceptable degree of risk to MCM forces. When operations are constrained by time, a greater degree of risk is generally required to accomplish the objective.

(3) **MCM Asset Availability.** MCM tactics are determined by the threat, environment, time, and available assets. The time required for MCM forces to arrive at the mined area and the time available for completion of MCM operations are key factors. AMCM forces usually provide short-notice, rapid response to any mining threat. These forces sacrifice some degree of effectiveness and stamina to maximize response capability. SMCM forces are often more effective but have relatively slow transit speeds and longer response times. For long distances, heavy-lift ships can transport SMCM units to the area more quickly with reduced SMCM wear and tear.

(4) **Amphibious Operations.** The performance of forcible entry assured access missions through the use of amphibious ships continues to evolve as designed according to espoused fundamentals in JP 3-02, *Amphibious Operations*. However, MCM and amphibious breaching is still required to support amphibious operations and must be synchronized within the overall amphibious task force (ATF) timeline. Planning a successful MCM or amphibious breach requires the combined efforts of the commander, amphibious task force (CATF), supported by the MCMC, the commander, landing force (CLF), and the MCMC. Early dialogue between these commanders will aid planners to identify detailed mission requirements. These considerations include:

(a) **Intelligence, Surveillance, and Reconnaissance.** A collection plan is a joint effort of the ATF intelligence organizations. Intelligence efforts should concentrate on identifying the type and location of the mine threat in the AOA, AOA characteristics, enemy locations, and intelligence on obstacles in the surf zone (SZ) and beyond.

(b) **Synchronization.** MCM and amphibious breaching operations require precise synchronization to ensure maximum effectiveness of supporting arms and to minimize the risk to friendly forces. The determination of the ATF general COA dictates the size and composition of the LF and the general location and number of lanes required. Lane requirements and obstacle construction will dictate size and composition of the breach force. Reverse planning should be used to ensure that actions at the obstacles support actions on the objective.

(c) **Breaching Fundamentals.** Suppression, obscuration, security, and reduction are applied to all amphibious breaching operations to ensure success when breaching against a defending enemy.

(d) **Organization.** ATF forces must be organized to quickly and effectively reduce obstacles and expedite LF movement to the objective. Forces should be task-organized into support, breach, and assault organizations.

(e) **Command and Control.** Unity of command is critical in MCM and in amphibious breaching operations. The CATF and the CLF share responsibility for MCM in the AOA, and the line of demarcation for their respective areas of responsibility for MCM is dependent on the particular topographic, hydrographic, meteorological, and tactical conditions of the AOA. As in other areas of amphibious warfare where the CATF and the CLF share planning responsibility, this line of demarcation should therefore be determined as part of the joint amphibious planning process. The CATF has overall responsibility for MW within the sea areas of the operational area. This includes the planning and execution of all facets of MW (working through the MIWC or MCMC as assigned) and providing the logistics support and force protection for MCM assets. The CATF is also responsible for conducting assault breaching operations from shallow water through the SZ and onto the beach, up to point or line of demarcation on the beach. The CLF is responsible for conducting mine and obstacle breaching and clearing operations landward from the CATF and the CLF mutually agreed upon line of demarcation on the beach, and for follow-on clearance operations on the beach.

(5) **Support Requirements.** Deployed MCM ships, helicopters, and EOD units are not self-sustaining. Communications, ordnance, recompression chambers, supply, personnel support, and petroleum, oils, and lubricants must be provided for these units. In addition, ships will require magnetic and acoustic calibration range services and intermediate maintenance support. Helicopter units will require hangar space, maintenance, and support equipment, either afloat or ashore depending upon the specific operation. Support may be provided to ships and EOD units by an assigned MCM support ship or an adjacent shore facility. Helicopter support may be provided by an adjacent airfield or by an air-capable MCM support ship. When operating near hostile enemy areas, force protection requirements exist for all MCM platforms.

(6) **Control Measures and Reporting.** The MCM operations report is used to exchange MCM tactical information between all components and joint headquarters. It provides the location and status of Service component MCM operations, including breaching and clearing. It is also used to request, task, plan, report, modify, and approve MCM operations, as appropriate. The report format is specified in Military Standard (MIL-STD)-6040, *US Message Text Formatting Program,* and listed in Appendix A, "Reporting."

(a) **Structured Operation Tasking MW Support.** The operation task (OPTASK) series of structured messages provide functional warfare area (e.g., MW, STRIKE, COMMS) specific policy and guidance. NMAWC is responsible for preparing and submitting the USN-wide OPTASK MW message and subsequent updates or changes to Third Fleet for review and promulgation by Commander, United States Fleet Forces Command (USFF)/Commander, United States Pacific Fleet (COMUSPACFLT) (NMAWC and Commander, Mobile Mine Assembly Group, provide input to the standing USN-wide OPTASK STRIKE message for mining operations). The standing USN-wide OPTASK MW is intended to be supplemented by numbered fleet commanders regarding mission and area of operations specifics, including issuance of fleet-level OPTASK MW and/or MCM addressing unique theater characteristics, command relationships, and operational-tactical direction. Prior to the commencement of an operation or exercise, an OPTASK MCM will normally be issued to the MCMC by the appropriate operational control authority. When required, the MCMC will prepare an additional OPTASK MCM to provide specific information to assigned MCM forces and any supported or supporting forces.

(b) **Mine Report.** The mine countermeasure report (MCMREP) is used by individual MCM organizations or a commander, task unit (CTU), to report results of MCM operations. The MCMC will specify the frequency for MCM assets or CTUs to submit MCMREPs.

Additional reports and reporting requirements for maritime mining and countermeasures can be found in NWP 3-15.2, Maritime Mine Countermeasures.

d. **Organizational Support**

(1) **Coast Guard Defense Forces.** Coast Guard Defense Forces East and West are commands established under the respective JFMCC to conduct maritime homeland defense missions for Commander, US Northern Command (USNORTHCOM), and Commander, US Pacific Command (USPACOM), including support for domestic MW operations.

(2) **NMAWC** is responsible to the Chief of Naval Operations for oversight of USN MW programs and, through the Navy chain of command for the integrated training and readiness of MW forces. The forces include AMCM, SMCM, UMCM, and MCMRONs, that can deploy on short notice to support CCDRs, as required. NMAWC supports these commanders in planning MCM exercises and operations.

e. **Operational Considerations.** When an enemy minefield is encountered, a number of decisions must be made. If the minefield is not on a primary SLOC or operational route, the best action may be to warn and divert shipping around the area. If the minefield is in an essential area, the decision must be made as to what type of MCM to employ. The number and types of mines, availability of MCM forces, and time will determine the type of MCM to employ. It may also be possible to counter a minefield in a critical area by sending forces over it (e.g., vertical envelopment or vertical resupply) rather than through or around it.

(1) **Integrated Operations.** Integrated MCM operations optimize available MCM assets and tactics to meet the needs of the mission. Consideration must be given to both

US Navy and Allied mine countermeasure forces during an exercise.

mutual support and mutual interference. For example, support from MCM helicopters may significantly reduce the risk to SMCM vessels if shallow moored mines and sensitive influence mines are swept before the SMCM employment. However, if influence sweeping is performed concurrent with EOD operations, this presents risk to EOD divers in proximity as a result of sweep-generated mine detonations. The MCMC must plan operations to exploit the strong capabilities of each MCM element and schedule events to accomplish the mission in the most efficient manner consistent with the risk directive.

(2) **Multinational Force Coordination.** Operations against enemy mining are often carried out by a multinational MCM effort. MCM operations may be conducted by several national forces in close proximity. To conduct such operations safely and efficiently, agreements to coordinate operational areas and communications, as a minimum, must be established to prevent mutual interference.

(3) **Q-Routes and Route Survey.** The Q-route system is a preplanned set of shipping routes that can be activated partially or totally by the area commander after determining that mining is imminent or has occurred. Activating Q-routes minimizes the area an MCMC has to clear to provide safe passage for shipping and reduces the force required to conduct MCM. Survey operations are conducted along Q-routes during peacetime to determine if the route is favorable for minehunting. If it is not, a change of route may be required. Once established, the route is surveyed to collect environmental and contact data to support wartime operations. The route is periodically surveyed to locate,

evaluate, and catalog contacts and environmental changes. This database can be used in conflict to determine if mining has occurred and, if it has, to reduce the time required to clear the route.

For additional information on maritime MCM capabilities, refer to Appendix E, "Maritime Mine Warfare and Mine Countermeasures Organization and Capabilities."

7. Service Considerations

a. **Army–Navy.** Naval MW includes mining and MCM in all sea areas, the littoral operating area in an amphibious operation to include the SZ and the beach (as determined in the amphibious planning process), and in certain cases may extend inland where waters are navigable from the sea. In short, if maritime assets are capable of conducting MCM in any waterway where Army craft need to navigate, it is likely that the maritime component commander will be directed to clear those mines. A mining threat in the US, at choke points along SLOCs, or at ports of debarkation can delay or completely halt the movement of material required to support overseas campaigns. Commander, joint task force, confronted by a mining threat, will request MCM assets through the CCDR. In some cases, combined MCM forces or forces from the North Atlantic Treaty Organization (NATO) or other allied nations may, after appropriate national coordination, provide MCM.

b. **Air Force–Navy.** The USAF plays two important roles in supporting MW forces (in addition to supporting offensive MCM). The first role is performed by USAF strike platforms. USAF bomber aircraft can deliver large quantities of mines per sortie at long distances from their bases, playing a critical part in accomplishing mining plans directed by joint commands. USAF strike platforms are also a key component of the assault breaching system in support of amphibious operations. The second USAF role is the Air Mobility Command's (AMC's) deployment of AMCM and UMCM forces, and MW C2 elements and the continuing delivery of critical repair parts via AMC aircraft. Under US Transportation Command direction, AMC integrates its effort in support of MCM with heavy sealift, whether of SMCM platforms or of personnel and materiel.

c. **Marine Corps–Navy.** During amphibious operations, MCM at sea—whether in the deep or shallow water where amphibious ships and their escorts operate, or in the very shallow water and SZ where assault craft bring troops and weapons to the beach—is conducted by a Navy MCMC. Normally, the MCMC is a subordinate and supporting commander to the CATF. MCM in the sea areas will be performed by a combination of the "MCM triad" of SMCM, AMCM, and UMCM assets; MCM in the very slow water will be performed by UMCM. When insertion of US Marine Corps forces (other than those already embarked on amphibious shipping) is accomplished by airlift of personnel to a benign location where they can be united with equipment stored on maritime pre-positioning ships squadron (MPSRON) ships, USN MCM assets may be required to assure access to seaports of debarkation for the use of those MPSRON vessels. In some situations the MPSRON ships will join the amphibious ships and be supported by MCM forces to establish logistics over-the-shore operations.

d. **United States Coast Guard (USCG).** The Commanders, Atlantic and Pacific Coast Guard areas, are USCG flag officers who are also designated Commanders, Coast Guard Defense Forces East and West, respectively, for the joint force maritime component commands USNORTHCOM and USPACOM. Coast Guard area commanders are empowered to assign appropriate USCG forces to the JFMCC to support MW operations. USCG assets are frequently included in exercises where mining and MCM are involved. Prior to initiating mining and MCM exercises in areas that are not regular USN operational areas, the Commander, Mine Warfare Command, must establish liaison with Commander, Coast Guard Defense Forces East or West, as appropriate. Commander, Coast Guard Defense Forces East or West, will notify subordinate USCG commands and coordinate USCG participation/support as required. USCG Juniper class buoy tenders have been and may be used to conduct survey operations in a number of scenarios using portable side-scan sonar equipment. USCG assets will likely support route survey and MCM forces conducting MW operations in US territorial waters in times of conflict.

For additional information on maritime mining capabilities, refer to Appendix D, "Maritime Mining Capabilities."

APPENDIX A
REPORTING

1. Land Forces Reports

Minefield reports will be submitted by the emplacing unit commanders through operations channels to the appropriate operations officer or operations directorate of a joint staff of the authorizing headquarters. That headquarters will integrate the reports with terrain intelligence and disseminate them through tactical intelligence. The reports should be sent by secure means. Once emplaced and activated, minefields are lethal and unable to distinguish between friendly forces and enemy. For this reason, positive control and continuous flow of information is necessary. Reporting, recording, and marking of minefields must be performed using methods that are consistent and well understood.

a. Enemy/Friendly (Allied Nation)/Minefield/Obstacle Report. Any detection, encounter, or knowledge of enemy minefields or mining activities must be reported by the fastest reliable means. The report is made to the next higher commander, and must include all known information about the minefield.

General Instructions: Use to report all obstacles on the battlefield after developing a report. Disseminate information and report to all command posts and units in the area of operation as soon as possible. From FM 6-99.2:

LINE 1 – DATE AND TIME _____ (DTG)

LINE 3 – EMPLACING UNIT_____ (Emplacing Unit, if Known (Enemy, Friendly Unit, Unit))

LINE 4 – APPROVING AUTHORITY (Approving Authority, if Required or Known)

LINE 5 – TARGET/OBSTACLE NO. (Target/Obstacle Number, if Required or Known)

LINE 6 – TYPE OF EMPLACING SYSTEM _____ (Type of Emplacing System, if Required or Known)

LINE 7 – TYPE MINES/OBSTACLES (Type Mines/Obstacle, if Known Include Width and Depth)

LINE 8 – TYPE MARKING SYSTEM (Type Minefield/Obstacle Marking System, if Emplaced)

LINE 9 – LIFE CYCLE DTG _____ (DTG of Life Cycle/Self-Destruct Time, if Known)

LINE 10 – CORNER LOCATIONS (UTM or Six-Digit Grid Coordinate With MGRS Grid Zone Designator of Corners)

LINE 11 – REDUCE _____ (Obstacle/Minefield Reduced, YES or NO)

LINE 12 – NO. OF LANES _____ (Number of Lanes)

LINE 13 – REDUCTION ASSET USED _____ (MICLIC, Mine Plow, Mine Roller, Demolitions, and so on)

LINE 14 – WIDTH _____ (Width of Lane)

LINE 15 – DEPTH _____ (Depth of Lane)

LINE 16 – GRID TO START OF LANE _____ (UTM or Six-Digit Grid
Coordinate With MGRS Grid
Zone Designator of Start of
Lane (Entrance))

LINE 17 – GRID TO END OF LANE _____ (UTM or Six-Digit Grid
Coordinate With MGRS Grid
Zone Designator of End of Lane
(Exit))

LINE 18 – LANE MARKING _____ (Type of Marking System, if
Emplaced)

LINE 19 – BYPASS_____ (YES or NO)

LINE 20 – BYPASS GRID (UTM or Six-Digit Grid
Coordinate With MGRS Grid
Zone Designator to Bypass)

LINE 21 – BARRIERS_____ (Concertina Wire, Pickets,
and/or Trenches, and any other
obstacle information necessary)

LINE 22 – NARRATIVE (Free Text for Additional
Information Required for
Clarification of Report)

LINE 23 – AUTHENTICATION _____ (Report Authentication)

b. **Scatterable Nonpersistent Minefield Reporting.** Accurate, timely, and uniform reporting and dissemination of scatterable nonpersistent minefield emplacement information is a must. Fluid and fast-moving tactical situations require that complete information on scatterable nonpersistent mine employment be known and passed on in a simple, rapid manner to all units that could be affected. The variety of emplacing systems and emplacing units preclude the use of locally devised reporting and dissemination methods. Scatterable nonpersistent minefields must also be recorded to facilitate clearing of possible UXO/duds. Shown below is a relatively simple reporting procedure that will be used for scatterable nonpersistent mines. It is applicable for all delivery systems and can be sent in a voice, digital, or hard copy mode. As in FM 6-99.2:

(1) Scatterable Minefield Warning

General Instructions: Use to request authority to execute a planned scatterable minefield (SCATMINE) obstacle. Use the SCATMINREQ to request authority to plan a SCATMINE obstacle and the SCATMINREC to record an executed SCATMINE obstacle.

LINE 1 – DATE AND TIME _____ (DTG)

LINE 2 – UNIT_____ (Unit Making Report)

LINE 3 – TGT/OBSTCL NO. _____ (Target/Obstacle Number, as
per Unit SOPs)

LINE 4 – EMPLACING SYSTEM _____ (Emplacing System (Volcano (Air or Ground), Artillery (Type), MOPMS, Air Delivered (Air Force), or Gator)

LINE 5 – ANTIVEHICULAR MINES _____ (Antitank Mines (YES or NO))

LINE 6 – ANTIPERSONNEL MINES_____ (Antipersonnel Mines (YES or NO))

LINE 7 – AIMING POINTS (Grid Coordinates of Aimpoints/Corner Points, if Required Due to Refinement When Authorized)

LINE 8 – SAFETY ZONE _____ (Size of Safety Zone)

LINE 9 – MINEFIELD MARKING _____ (Type of Marking, if Applicable)

LINE 10 – LIFE CYCLE_____ (DTG of Life Cycle)

LINE 11 – ACTIONS _____ (Actions Taken by Personnel Involved)

LINE 12 – NARRATIVE_____ (Free Text for Additional Information Required for Clarification of Report)

LINE 13 – AUTHENTICATION _____ (Report Authentication)

(2) Scatterable Minefield Request

General Instructions: Use to request authority to plan emplacement of SCATMINE. IAW unit SOPs or the SCATMINE planning and execution policy, units will prepare and submit SCATMINREQ in enough time to allow the request to be staffed at the appropriate level and approval or disapproval returned to the requesting unit. Once a unit receives permission to plan a SCATMINE obstacle, it must still receive release authority before proceeding. This process is normally given when a scatterable minefield warning (SCATMINWARN) is sent 30 minutes prior to execution and the higher commander acknowledges and approves the release. Once the minefield is in place, a minefield/obstacle report (SCATMINREC) is sent to register the minefield. This is key, as the minefield may be on a unit boundary or beyond the FLOT As in FM 6-99.2:

LINE 1 – DATE AND TIME _____ (DTG)

LINE 2 – UNIT_____ (Unit Making Report)

LINE 3 – TGT/OBSTCL NO. (Target/Obstacle Number, as per Unit SOPs)

LINE 4 – EMPLACING SYSTEM _____ (Emplacing System (Volcano (Air or Ground), Artillery (Type), MOPMS, Air Delivered (Air Force), or Gator)

LINE 5 - ANTIVEHICULAR MINES _____ (YES or NO)

LINE 6 - ANTIPERSONNEL MINES _____ (YES or NO)

LINE 7 – ATTITUDE _____ (Attitude of Minefield)

LINE 8 – DIMENSIONS_____ (Dimensions of Minefield)

LINE 9 – AIMPOINTS (Number of Aimpoints/Corner Points With Grid Coordinates)

LINE 10 – SAFETY ZONE _____ (Size of Safety Zone)

LINE 11 – MINEFIELD MARKING _____ (Type of Marking, if Applicable)

LINE 12 - UNIT OBSERVING _____ (Unit Observing)

LINE 13 – MISSION _____ (Task, Purpose, and Intent)

LINE 14 - LIFE CYCLE _____ (DTG of Life Cycle Planned)

LINE 15 – ACTIONS _____ (Actions Taken by Personnel Involved)

LINE 16 – NARRATIVE (Free Text for Additional Information Required for Clarification of Report)

LINE 17 – AUTHENTICATION _____ (Report Authentication)

(3) Scatterable Minefield Record

GENERAL INSTRUCTIONS: Use to report emplacement of SCATMINE. IAW unit SOPs or SCATMINE planning and execution policy, units will prepare and submit SCATMINREC in enough time to allow the request to be disseminated to all affected units. Once executed, it is critical to report each obstacle as a separate SCATMINREC to ensure it gains immediate visibility. (Placing SCATMINREC in the obstacle database, which is how most of the normal obstacles will be reported, slows dissemination.) This is especially important if the obstacle is on a unit boundary or beyond the FLOT. As in FM 6-99.2:

LINE 1 – DATE AND TIME _____ (DTG)

LINE 2 – UNIT_____ (Unit Making Report)

LINE 3 – TGT/OBSTCL NO. _____ (Target/Obstacle Number, as per Unit SOPs)

LINE 4 – EMPLACING SYSTEM _____ (Emplacing System (Volcano (Air or Ground), Artillery (Type), MOPMS, Air Delivered (Air Force), or Gator)

LINE 5 - ANTIVEHICULAR MINES _____ (YES or NO)

LINE 6 - ANTIPERSONNEL MINES _____ (YES or NO)

LINE 7 - LIFE CYCLE _____ (DTG of Life Cycle Planned (Emplacement DTG and Self-Destruct/Self-Deactivating DTG))

LINE 8 – AIMPOINTS _____ (Aimpoints/Center Point of the Minefield)

a. _____ (UTM or Six-Digit Grid of One Corner)

b. _____ (UTM or Six-Digit Grid of One Corner)

c. _____ (UTM or Six-Digit Grid of One Corner)

d. _____ (UTM or Six-Digit Grid of One Corner)

LINE 9 – AIMPOINTS _____ (Aimpoints/Center Point of the Minefield)

a. _____ (UTM or Six-Digit Grid of One Corner)

b. _____ (UTM or Six-Digit Grid of One Corner)

c. _____ (UTM or Six-Digit Grid of One Corner)

d. _____ (UTM or Six-Digit Grid of One Corner)

LINE 10 – AIMPOINTS _____ (Aimpoints/Center Point of the Minefield)

a. _____ (UTM or Six-Digit Grid of One Corner)

b. _____ (UTM or Six-Digit Grid of One Corner)

c. _____ (UTM or Six-Digit Grid of One Corner)

d. _____ (UTM or Six-Digit Grid of One Corner)

LINE 11 – AIMPOINTS _____ (Aimpoints/Center Point of the Minefield)

a. _____ (UTM or Six-Digit Grid of One Corner)

b. _____ (UTM or Six-Digit Grid of One Corner)

c. _____ (UTM or Six-Digit Grid of One Corner)

d. _____ (UTM or Six-Digit Grid of One Corner)

LINE 12 – AIMPOINTS _____ (Aimpoints/Center Point of the Minefield)

LINE 13 – AIMPOINTS _____ (Aimpoints/Center Point of the Minefield)

LINE 14 – EMPLACING _____ (Unit Emplacing Mines and Report Number)

LINE 15 – SAFETY ZONE _____ (Size of Safety Zone)

LINE 16 – MINEFIELD MARKING _____ (Type of Marking, if Applicable)

LINE 17 – APPROVING AUTHORITY _____ (Approving Authority Commander)

LINE 18 – POC THIS REPORT _____ (Person Completing This Report)

LINE 19 – ACTIONS _____ (Actions Taken by Personnel Involved)

| LINE 20 – NARRATIVE_____ | (Free Text for Additional Information Required for Clarification of Report) |
| LINE 21 – AUTHENTICATION _____ | (Report Authentication) |

    c. Unexploded Ordnance/Explosive Remnants of War Reporting. The UXO SPOTREP is a detailed, swift, two-way reporting system that makes clear where the UXO hazard areas are, what their priorities are, and which units are affected by them. The report is used to request help in handling a UXO hazard that is beyond a unit's ability to handle and that affects the unit's mission. This report helps commanders set priorities based on the battlefield situation. The UXO SPOTREP is the first-echelon report that is sent when a UXO is encountered. The report consists of nine lines and is sent by the fastest means available. As in FM 4-30.51 / MCRP 3-17.2A:

LINE 1 – DATE TIME GROUP _____	DTG item was discovered
LINE 2 – REPORTING ACTIVITY_____	(Unit identification code) and location (grid of UXO).
LINE 3 – CONTACT METHOD _____	Radio frequency, call sign, point of contact and telephone number.
LINE 4 – TYPE OF ORDNANCE	Dropped, projected, placed or thrown. If available, supply the subgroup. Give the size of the hazard area.
LINE 5 – CBRN CONTAMINATION _____	Be as specific as possible.
LINE 6 – RESOURCES THREATENED _____	Report any equipment, facilities, or other assets that are threatened.
LINE 7 – IMPACT ON MISSION	Provide a short description of current tactical situation and how the presence of UXO affects mission.
LINE 8 – PROTECTIVE MEASURES	Describe any measures you have taken to protect personnel and equipment.
LINE 9 – RECOMMENDED PRIORITY_____	Recommend a priority for response by EOD or engineers.

APPENDIX B
LAND MOBILITY CAPABILITIES

1. Operational Environment

The operational environment includes significant challenges to both mobility and maneuver. Within the threat dimension, potential adversaries span the spectrum from modern heavy conventional forces to unconventional forces employing asymmetric means. Potential challenges to maneuver range from conventional obstacles and mines employed in depth to booby traps, and other EHs employed in improvised and adaptive attacks. Adversaries may seek refuge in terrain that by its nature and remoteness challenges maneuver. They will use complex terrain and urban areas to disperse US and multinational forces and limit many of our capabilities. Support to movement and maneuver tends to be focused at the tactical and lower operational levels in support of combat maneuver. It is primarily related to forces operating on land. Mobility support is applicable at all echelons and for all military forces. The focus of this appendix is on providing a concise discussion of enemy countermobility capabilities and their employment of land mines and other EHs. It includes a discussion of the US units and potential capabilities to provide mobility and support to movement and maneuver against these countermobility capabilities.

a. **Land Mines.** Whether buried conventionally in patterns, emplaced on the surface in seemingly random fashion, or intentionally scattered, land mines will likely be present in prolific numbers on the battlefield. Potential adversaries with conventional military capabilities will employ large numbers of land mines to offset our maneuver advantages. Highly developed adversaries may employ large numbers of scatterable mines. Less developed adversaries are likely to employ more conventional mines and other EHs in lieu of scatterable mines. Terrorists will obtain and employ land mines in any manner possible to inflict losses on our friendly forces as well as civilians. Their most likely choice will be EHs to include IEDs rather than mines, but their use of mines remains a very real possibility. The numbers and types of land mines available to potential adversaries are extensive and include APLs and AVLs with numerous types of firing mechanisms (see FM 3-34.210/MCRP 3-17.2D, *Explosive Hazards Operations*; Training Circular [TC] 20-32-3, *Foreign Mine Handbook [Balkan States]*; TC 20-32-4, *Foreign Mine Handbook [Asia]*; TC 20-32-5, *Commander's Reference Guide: Land Mine and Explosive Hazards [Iraq]*). Conventional employment of mines will typically be integrated with other obstacles such as wire and tank ditches to create complex obstacles.

b. **Explosive Hazards.** An EH is any hazard containing an explosive component. FM 3-90.119/MCIP 3-17.01, *Combined Arms Improvised Explosive Device (IED) Defeat Operations*, describes EHs currently encountered on the battlefield in five categories: UXO (including land mines), booby traps (some booby traps are nonexplosive), IEDs, captured enemy ammunition, and bulk explosives. Information in this manual focuses on the enemy's employment of EHs as a direct challenge to friendly freedom of maneuver. **IEDs and UXO are the two types of EHs that are of greatest concern for movement and maneuver.**

See FM 3-34.210/ MCRP 3-17.2D, Explosive Hazards Operations, *for additional supporting information.*

(1) **The Improvised Explosive Device System.** IEDs are not a new phenomenon, but recent use of IEDs has greatly expanded the methods in which they are used and the types of materials used to create them, which poses an increasing challenge to our freedom of maneuver. The improvised version can be almost anything containing explosive material and initiator. It is an improvised device that is designed to cause death or injury by using explosives alone or in combination with other materials—to include projectiles, toxic chemicals, biological toxins, or radiological material. IEDs can be produced in varying sizes, functioning methods, containers, and delivery methods. Commercial or military explosives, homemade explosives, or military ordnance and ordnance components can be used to make them. IEDs are primarily conventional high-explosive charges, also known as homemade bombs. A chemical and biological agent, or even radiological material, may be included to add to the destructive power and the psychological effect of the device. They are unique because the IED builder has had to improvise with the materials at hand. Designed to defeat a specific target or type of target, they generally become more difficult to detect and protect against as they become more sophisticated. The sophistication of IEDs varies greatly from a crude design fabricated from common materials to premanufactured kits, and ranging in size from a cigarette pack to a large vehicle. IEDs can be detonated in numerous ways including radio control, heat/sound/motion sensor, command wire, and victim initiated. The degree of sophistication depends on the ingenuity of the designer and the tools and materials available. Cached, stockpiled munitions within the theater of operations may provide the explosive materials to would-be enemy bombers.

For more information on IEDs and countering IEDs, see JP 3-15.1, Counter-Improvised Explosive Device Operations.

(2) **Unexploded Explosive Ordnance.** UXO includes ordnance items that have been fired, projected, dropped, or placed in such a way that they propose a hazard to personnel or property. Whether in an area by design or accident, these items have not yet fully functioned or detonated and are hazards. UXO poses the risk of injury or death to personnel but also can pose a challenge to maneuver along a key route or within a significant area.

See FM 3-100.38/MCRP 3-17.2B/NTTP 3-02.4.1/AFTTP(I) 3-2.12, Multi-Service Tactics, Techniques, and Procedures for Unexploded Explosive Ordnance Operations, *and FM 4-30.16/MCRP 3-17.2C/NTTP 3-02.5/AFTTP(I) 3-2.32,* Multi-Service Tactics, Techniques, and Procedures for Explosive Ordnance Disposal in a Joint Environment.

2. **Staff Integration for Support to Movement and Maneuver**

Each maneuver force echelon down to the BCT and the RCT level has organic staff capability (engineers, military police [MP], chemical, biological, radiological, and nuclear [CBRN], and others such as EOD when augmented) to integrate their collective combat support (CS) mobility capabilities into the combined arms fight. These CS planners are the primary members of the battle staff responsible for understanding and integrating mobility capabilities to support movement and maneuver. Those capabilities may be organic to or augment the maneuver force. These staff members synchronize their collective capabilities to support the needs of the maneuver commander and enable movement and maneuver for the force.

3. Mobility Units and Capabilities

a. Army

(1) **Organic Mobility Units and Capabilities.** The Army is a brigade-based force. The major combat and support capabilities a brigade needs for most operations are organic to its structure. Each BCT has one or more organic combat engineer companies whose primary focus is supporting combined arms mobility operations. Other engineer elements in the BCT include a terrain team and engineer planners. See JP 3-34, *Joint Engineer Operations*, for more information about these units and their capabilities. Other mobility support assets within the BCT include reconnaissance elements and, in some cases, MP platoons. Additional information on the structure of each of the BCTs and their subordinate units can be found in FM 3-90.6, *Brigade Combat Team*, and FM 3-90.61, *Brigade Special Troops Battalion*. Additional information on the capabilities and structure of the organic combat engineers can be found in FM 3-34, *Engineer Operations*, and Army Tactics, Techniques, and Procedures (ATTP) 3-34.22, *Engineer Operations-Brigade Combat Team and Below*.

(2) **Augmenting Mobility Units and Capabilities.** The organic structure of the BCT does not include all the combat engineer mobility support needed to conduct mobility operations. The BCT has organic engineer elements as shown previously in this appendix, but may need additional breaching, clearing, gap crossing, or other selected capabilities based on mission requirements. The BCT commander and staff must identify and address required capability shortfalls through mission analysis and augmentation.

(a) **Engineer Augmentation.** Organic engineer capability within the BCTs may require augmentation to support mobility operations. The engineer force pool includes engineer units not organic to a BCT or embedded in a headquarters staff. For combined arms breaching operations, the BCT will generally require augmentation of one or two mobility augmentation companies, a combat engineer company, and additional route clearance platoons. The type and number of augmentation units required will vary with METT-T. For a gap crossing operation, the BCT would require the augmentation listed above plus at least one multi-role bridge company. In clearance operations, the BCT may be augmented by numerous clearance and combat engineer elements (and perhaps a mine dog detection team). Engineer units and capabilities likely to augment the BCT in mobility operations include the combat engineer company, mobility augmentation company, clearance company, engineer support company, explosive hazards coordination cell (EHCC), and engineer mine dog detection unit. The EHCC's mission is to predict, track, distribute information on, and mitigate EHs within the theater that affect force application focused logistics, survivability, and awareness of the operational environment. The EHCC maintains an EH database, conducts pattern analysis, investigates mine and IED strikes, and tracks UXO hazard areas. The cell provides technical advice on the mitigation of EH, including the development of TTP, and provides training updates to field units. For more information about these units, see JP 3-34, *Joint Engineer Operations*. Army, Marine Corps, and Navy units may form engineer reconnaissance teams (ERTs). An ERT is not an engineer unit but rather an engineer capability. The current engineer force structure does not provide for engineer personnel or equipment dedicated to reconnaissance efforts. However, experience has shown that employment of engineers in a reconnaissance role enhances the effectiveness of reconnaissance in support of mobility operations. Because an engineer unit has limited assets to draw from, the formation of ERTs can subsequently degrade the capabilities of the organization from which they are drawn. The commander must understand the trade-offs between using engineer assets in a reconnaissance role versus using them in other roles.

(b) **Other Mobility Support Augmentation**

1. **EOD** units provide the capability to neutralize hazards from conventional UXO, IED, CBRN and high-yield explosives, and associated materials that present a threat to operations, installations, personnel, and/or material. EOD forces also may dispose of hazardous foreign or US ammunition, UXO, individual mines, booby-trapped mines, and chemical mines. EOD forces serve as a combat multiplier by neutralizing UXO that is restricting freedom of movement and denying access to supplies, facilities, and other critical assets. EOD forces equip, train, and organize to support tactical land forces across the range of military operations.

2. **Rotary and fixed wing joint aviation assets** will provide critical augmentation to the BCT to support mobility operations. Aviation support will augment the BCT reconnaissance and fire support capability, provide airborne mine dispensing capability, support the BCTs ability to maneuver and bypass obstacles.

3. **CBRN.** CBRN assets that can support the BCT and its engineers include:

a. CBRN Reconnaissance Platoon (infantry BCT [IBCT]). This platoon conducts dismounted CBRN reconnaissance and consequence management support.

b. CBRN Reconnaissance Platoon (heavy BCT [HBCT]). This platoon conducts mounted CBRN reconnaissance and can conduct biological surveillance if properly equipped.

c. CBRN Reconnaissance Platoon (Stryker BCT [SBCT]). This platoon conducts mounted CBRN reconnaissance and can conduct biological surveillance if properly equipped.

d. CBRN Decontamination Platoon (Heavy). This platoon conducts thorough equipment and troop decontamination.

e. CBRN Decontamination Platoon (Light). This platoon conducts operational level decontamination.

f. CBRN Platoon (Obscuration) (Mechanized). This platoon conducts sustainment and temporary obscuration.

g. CBRN Platoon (Obscuration) (Wheeled). This platoon conducts sustainment and temporary obscuration and military deception operations.

4. **CA teams** execute a variety of activities such as civil-military relations, military civic action, population and resource control, and care of refugees. CA team interaction with the local authorities or populace can be employed to gather terrain and OBSTINT and to control access to routes or areas in support of mobility operations. CA elements assess the needs of civil authorities; act as an interface between civil authorities and the military supporting agency and as liaison to the civil populace. CA units develop population and resource control measures and coordinate with international support agencies. CA personnel are regionally oriented and possess cultural and linguistic knowledge of countries in each region.

5. **Tactical-level military information support operations (MISO) supports battles and engagements** by bringing psychological pressure on hostile forces and by persuading civilians to assist the tactical supported commander in achieving the commander's objectives. Another primary focus of MISO is to reduce interference with military operations. MISO personnel assist the commander by encouraging civilians to avoid military operations, installations, and convoys. MISO teams support counterterrorism by decreasing popular support for terrorists, terrorist activities, and terrorist causes.

b. **Marine Corps.** The Marine Corps deploys units based on the MAGTF construct. Each MAGTF consists of four elements: the command element, ground combat element (GCE), aviation combat element (ACE), and logistics combat element (LCE).

(1) The GCE of all MAGTFs includes task-organized combat engineer detachments that provide mobility and countermobility support. They range in size from a platoon reinforced, company reinforced, to entire combat engineer battalion (CEB).

(2) Combat engineer platoons and companies can be reinforced by elements of the CEB's mobility assault company (MAC) and engineer support company. MAC consists of six route, reconnaissance, and clearance platoons and one assault breaching platoon. Engineer support company consists of heavy equipment and motor transport assets to transport it.

(3) The LCE of all MAGTFs includes task-organized engineer support battalion (ESB) detachments that provide general support, general engineering, and combat engineering (mobility/countermobility). Engineer platoons and companies can be reinforced by elements of engineer support company, bridge company, and EOD company.

For additional information about Marine Corps engineer units and capabilities, see JP 3-34, Joint Engineer Operations.

Intentionally Blank

APPENDIX C
LAND COUNTERMOBILITY CAPABILITIES

1. Employment of Barriers, Obstacles, and Mines

As with the support of mobility, countermobility operations will be affected by the operational environment. Countermobility execution is primarily the responsibility of combat engineers, although many other capabilities are integrated with their efforts. The engineer and the tactical commander must decide early in the planning process how to best position obstacles (including mines and other obstructions) to increase the effectiveness of friendly fire and maneuver and deny or channel the maneuver of the enemy. Combined arms obstacle integration is a necessary function of countermobility operations. Countermobility operations are also a part of support to movement and maneuver and have the likelihood of requiring and competing for many of the same combat engineer assets that are also required for mobility or survivability operations. Properly integrated obstacles, obscurants, and fires help to wrest the initiative from the enemy and deny him his objectives.

a. **Barriers.** A barrier is a coordinated series of obstacles designed or employed to channel, direct, restrict, delay, or stop the movement of an opposing force and to impose additional losses in personnel, time, and equipment on the opposing force. Barriers can exist naturally, be man-made, or be a combination of both. The construction of barriers may require extensive engineer support, time, and materials and is more likely to employ general engineers in their construction than obstacles or minefields.

b. **Obstacles.** An obstacle is any obstruction designed or employed to disrupt, fix, turn, or block the movement of an opposing force. They are also employed to impose additional losses in personnel, time, and equipment on the opposing force. Obstacles can exist naturally, be man-made, or be a combination of the two. The effectiveness of obstacles is enhanced considerably when covered by observation and fire. Obstacles include abatis, AVL ditches, blown bridges, built-up areas, minefields, rivers, road craters, terrain, and wire. As mentioned above, mines are employed in combination with other obstacles to create complex obstacles.

c. **Land Mines.** Mines are explosive devices that are emplaced to kill, destroy, or incapacitate enemy personnel and/or equipment. They can be employed in quantity within a specified area to form a minefield, or they can be used individually to reinforce nonexplosive obstacles. They can also be emplaced individually or in groups to demoralize an enemy force. Mines may be emplaced by hand or delivered by other means. A minefield is an area of ground that contains mines or an area of ground that is perceived to contain mines (a phony minefield). Minefields may contain scatterable mines and/or networked munitions. By executive order, US forces may no longer use non-self-destructing APLs, except to train personnel engaged in demining and countermine operations. The use of the M18A1 Claymore used in the command-detonation mode is not restricted under international law or executive order. Tactical minefield effects include disrupt, turn, fix, and block. Minefields are used to:

(1) Produce a vulnerability to enemy maneuver that can be exploited by friendly forces.

(2) Cause the enemy to piecemeal his forces.

(3) Interfere with enemy C2.

(4) Inflict damage to enemy personnel and equipment.

(5) Exploit the capabilities of other weapon systems by delaying enemy forces in an engagement area.

(6) Protect friendly forces from enemy maneuver and infiltration.

d. **Types of Minefields.** There are four general types of minefields: protective, tactical, nuisance, and phony. Each type is determined by its distinct operational environment purpose. Therefore, minefields are employed differently and they target the enemy in unique ways that support the overall concept of the operations.

(1) **Protective minefields** are employed to protect the force, equipment, supplies, and facilities from enemy attacks or other threats. Protective minefields are usually employed and emplaced at the small-unit level (platoon or company/team). The authority to emplace protective minefields is normally delegated to the company/team commander. In some cases, such as a hasty defense, protective minefields are emplaced on short notice by units that use mines from their basic load or local stock. More commonly, protective minefields are used as part of a unit's deliberate defense. The mines are emplaced so that they are easy to detect and recover by the emplacing unit. Much like final protective fires, protective minefields provide the defender with close-in protection during the enemy's final assault. Protective minefields serve two purposes. First, they impose a delay on an attacker that allows the defender time to break contact as the unit displaces to another battle position. Secondly, they break up the enemy's assault to complete its destruction. The composition of a protective minefield is driven by the vulnerability of the defender.

(2) **Tactical minefields** directly affect the enemy's maneuver in a way that gives the defending force a positional advantage. Tactical minefields may be employed by themselves or in conjunction with other types of tactical obstacles. They attack the enemy's maneuver by disrupting its combat formations, interfering with its C2, reducing its ability to mass fires, causing it to prematurely commit limited breaching resources, and reducing its ability to reinforce. The defender masses fires and maneuver to exploit the positional advantage created in part by tactical obstacles. Tactical minefields add an offensive dimension to the defense. They are a commander's tool for recapturing and maintaining the initiative that is normally afforded to an attacker. Combined with fires, tactical obstacles force the attacker to conform to the defender's plan. Tactical minefields may be emplaced during offensive operations to protect exposed flanks, isolate the objective area, deny enemy counterattack routes, and disrupt enemy retrograde.

(3) **Nuisance minefields** impose caution on enemy forces and disrupt, delay, and sometimes weaken or destroy follow-on echelons. Nuisance minefields are a form of tactical

minefields. Once nuisance minefields are emplaced, they do not require cover by observation or direct fire. Nuisance minefields are usually irregular in size and shape; they can be a single group of mines or a series of mined areas. They can be used to reinforce existing obstacles and can also be rapidly emplaced on main avenues of approach. Self-destruct/self-deactivating mines, scatterable mines, and/or networked munitions may be used in nuisance minefields.

(4) **Phony minefields** deceive the enemy about the exact location of real minefields. They cause the attacker to question his decision to breach and may cause him to expend his reduction assets wastefully. Phony minefields may be employed in conjunction with other minefields, but should be used only after the enemy has become mine-sensitive. The success of phony minefields depends on the enemy's state of mind. The bluff succeeds best when the enemy is mine-conscious and has already suffered the consequences of a mine encounter. A fear of mines can quickly evolve into paranoia and break the momentum of the enemy's attack. Therefore, phony minefields are normally employed in conjunction with real minefields and are seldom employed alone. Once the enemy has become mine-conscious, phony minefields may produce considerable tactical effects with very little investment in time, labor, and material. Phony minefields may also be used to extend the front and depth of live minefields when mines or labor are in short supply or when time is restricted. They may be used to conceal minefield gaps through live minefields. **There is no guarantee that phony minefields will achieve their purpose.**

e. It is important to distinguish the difference between the types of minefield and the means of emplacement. Volcano, Modular Pack Mine System, standard-pattern, and row mining are not types of minefields; they are just some of the means used to emplace tactical, nuisance, and protective minefields. They may also be the method of emplacement that is replicated by a phony minefield.

f. **Types of Mines**

(1) **Anti-Vehicle Mines.** AVLs are designed to immobilize or destroy vehicles and their occupants.

(a) **Types of Kills.** An AVL produces a mobility kill (M-Kill) or a catastrophic kill (K-Kill). An M-Kill destroys one or more of the vehicle's vital drive components (for example, breaks a track on a tank) and immobilizes the target. An M-Kill does not always destroy the weapon system and the crew; they may continue to function. In a K-Kill, the weapon system or the crew is destroyed.

(b) **Types of Sensing.** Anti-vehicle fuzes fall into three design categories:

1. **Track-width.** Usually pressure-actuated, requiring contact with the wheels or tracks of a vehicle.

2. **Full-width.** Activated by several methods—acoustics, magnetic influence, tilt-rod, radio frequency, infrared sensor, command, or vibration. Tilt-rod or magnetic-influence fuzes are the most common. Full-width fuzes are designed to be effective over the entire target width and can cause a K-Kill from penetration and spalling

metal or from secondary explosions. When a full-width fuze is activated solely by contact with the wheels or tracks of the target vehicle, it usually causes an M-Kill because most of the energy is absorbed by the wheels or tracks.

3. **Off-route.** Designed to be placed along the side of a route likely to be taken by armored vehicles. It has numerous fuzing possibilities, including infrared, seismic, break wire, and magnetic. It produces an M-Kill or a K-Kill, depending on the location of the target at the time of mine detonation.

(c) **Types of Warheads.** AVLs can be identified by their warheads:

1. Blast AVLs derive their effectiveness from the force generated by high-explosive detonation. They usually produce an M-Kill when the blast damages the track or the vehicle, but a K-Kill is also possible.

2. Shaped-charge mines use a directed-energy warhead. A shaped charge is formed by detonating an explosive charge behind a cone of dense metal or other material. Upon detonation, the cone collapses and forms a metal slug and a gaseous metal jet that penetrate the target. A K-Kill is probable if the crew or ammunition compartment is hit.

3. Explosive-formed penetrating mines have an explosive charge with a metal plate in front. Upon detonation, the plate forms into an inverted disk, a slug, or a long rod. A K-Kill is probable if the crew or ammunition compartment is hit.

(2) **AP Mines**

(a) **Types of Kills.** AP mines can kill or incapacitate their victims. The injuries and deaths they cause commit medical resources, degrade unit morale, and damage nonarmored vehicles. Some types of AP mines may break or damage the track on armored vehicles.

(b) **Types of Sensing.** AP mines can be fuzed in many ways, to include pressure, seismic, wire, or command detonation:

1. Pressure fuzes usually activate an AP mine when a load is placed on the fuze.

2. Seismic fuzes activate an AP mine when the sensor detects vibrations.

3. Trip wires or break wires activate an AP mine when something disturbs barely visible wires.

4. Command-detonated mines are activated by an individual when he detects the enemy in the mines' blast area.

(c) **Types of Effects.** AP mines contain five types of effects:

<u>1</u>. **Blast.** Cripples the foot or leg of an individual who steps on it; can also burst the tires of a wheeled vehicle that passes over it.

<u>2</u>. **Bounding fragmentation.** Throws a canister into the air; the canister bursts and scatters shrapnel throughout the immediate area. US policy prohibits the use of bounding fragmentation APLs.

<u>3</u>. **Direct-fragmentation.** Propels fragments in the general direction of enemy soldiers.

<u>4</u>. **Stake-fragmentation.** Bursts and scatters shrapnel in all general directions.

<u>5</u>. **Chemical.** Disperses a chemical agent to whoever activates it; contaminates the surrounding area.

(3) **AHDs.** AHDs perform the function of a mine fuze if someone attempts to tamper with the mine. They are intended to prevent moving or removing the mine, not to prevent reduction of the minefield by enemy dismounts. An AHD usually consists of an explosive charge that is connected to, placed next to, or manufactured in the mine. The device can be attached to the mine body and activated by a wire that is attached to a firing mechanism. US policy no longer allows employment of persistent mines of any type; therefore, we will not put AHDs on conventional mines. Other countries continue to employ AHDs on AVLs and APLs. Some mines have extra fuze wells that make it easier to install AHDs. An AHD does not have to be attached to the mine; it can be placed underneath the mine. Mines with AHDs are sometimes incorrectly called booby-trapped mines.

2. Staff Integration of Countermobility and Support to Movement and Maneuver

Each maneuver force echelon down to the BCT and the RCT level has organic staff capability (engineers, MP, CBRN, and others such as EOD when augmented) to integrate their collective CS countermobility capabilities into the combined arms fight. These CS planners are the primary members of the battle staff responsible for understanding and integrating countermobility capabilities to support movement and maneuver. Those capabilities may be organic to or augment the maneuver force. These staff members synchronize their collective capabilities to support the needs of the maneuver commander and assure movement and maneuver for the force. Countermobility focuses on denying the enemy movement and maneuver as well as enabling freedom of movement and maneuver of the friendly force.

3. Countermobility Units and Capabilities

a. Army

(1) **Organic Countermobility Units and Capabilities.** Modular force brigades are strategically flexible. The major combat and support capabilities a brigade needs for most operations are organic to its structure. Each BCT has one or more organic combat engineer companies, whose primary focus includes supporting combined arms

countermobility operations. Other engineer elements in the BCT include a terrain team and engineer planners. See JP 3-34, *Joint Engineer Operations*, for more information about these units and their capabilities. Other countermobility support assets within the BCT include reconnaissance elements and, in some cases, MP platoons. Additional information on the structure of BCTs and their subordinate units can be found in FM 3-90.6, *Brigade Combat Team*, and FM 3-90.61, *Brigade Special Troops Battalion*. Additional information on the capabilities and structure of the organic combat engineers and those engineer organizations and capabilities likely to augment each of the BCTs can be found in FM 3-34, *Engineer Operations*, and ATTP 3-34.22, *Engineer Operations—Brigade Combat Team and Below*.

(2) **Augmenting Countermobility Units and Capabilities.** The organic structure of the BCT does not include all the combat engineer and other elements needed to conduct countermobility operations. The BCTs have organic engineer elements as shown previously in this appendix, but may need additional capabilities based on mission requirements. The BCT commander and staff must identify and address required capability shortfalls through augmentation.

(a) **Engineer Augmentation.** Organic engineer capability within the BCTs will require augmentation to support countermobility operations exceeding their close CS capability. The engineer company within the HBCT is equipped with four Volcano mine dispensers. The single engineer company of the SBCT is equipped with three Volcano mine dispensers, while the IBCT has no organic Volcano mine dispensing equipment. The engineer force pool includes engineer units not organic to a BCT or embedded in a headquarters staff. For a deliberate defense, the BCT will generally require augmentation of an engineer battalion headquarters with countermobility and survivability augmentation that includes mobility assault, sapper, and engineer support companies to perform countermobility tasks in support of the BCT. The type and number of augmentation units required will vary with METT-T. Engineer units and capabilities likely to augment the BCT in countermobility operations include the **sapper company, mobility augmentation company,** and **engineer support company.**

For more information about these units, see JP 3-34, Joint Engineer Operations.

(b) **Other Countermobility Support Augmentation**

<u>1</u>. Rotary- and fixed-wing joint aviation assets will provide critical augmentation to the BCT to support countermobility operations. Aviation support will augment the BCT reconnaissance capability, add fire support capability including the possible employment of scatterable mines, and support the BCT's ability to maneuver in relation to the natural or emplaced obstacles.

<u>2</u>. Indirect fires are integrated with the countermobility effort to magnify the effects of the barriers, obstacles, and mines. The organic artillery battalion in each of the BCTs will be augmented or reinforced to provide the requisite fire support for the BCT.

<u>3</u>. CBRN assets that can support the BCT and its engineers include:

      <u>a.</u> CBRN Reconnaissance Platoon (IBCT). This platoon conducts dismounted CBRN reconnaissance and consequence management support.

      <u>b.</u> CBRN Reconnaissance Platoon (HBCT). This platoon conducts mounted CBRN reconnaissance and can conduct biological surveillance if properly equipped.

      <u>c.</u> CBRN Reconnaissance Platoon (SBCT). This platoon conducts mounted CBRN reconnaissance and can conduct biological surveillance if properly equipped.

      <u>d.</u> CBRN Decontamination Platoon (Heavy). This platoon conducts thorough equipment and troop decontamination.

      <u>e.</u> CBRN Decontamination Platoon (Light). This platoon conducts operational level decontamination.

      <u>f.</u> CBRN Platoon (Obscuration) (Mechanized). This platoon conducts sustainment and temporary obscuration.

      <u>g.</u> CBRN Platoon (Obscuration) (Wheeled). This platoon conducts sustainment and temporary obscuration and military deception operations.

  b. **US Marine Corps.** The GCE of all MAGTFs include task-organized combat engineer detachments that provide mobility and countermobility support. These detachments are sourced from the Marine division's CEB. The ESB of the Marine logistics group provides general engineering support in support of MAGTF countermobility requirements. The Marine wing support squadron of the ACE provides limited countermobility support, especially at MAGTF air facilities.

For additional information about Marine Corps engineer units and capabilities, see JP 3-34, Joint Engineer Operations.

Intentionally Blank

APPENDIX D
MARITIME MINING CAPABILITIES

1. The Minefield

a. The Minefield Compared with Other Weapons

(1) In naval warfare, a minefield is defined as an area of water containing mines emplaced with or without a defined pattern. If the field is not declared or the mine emplacement operation goes unobserved, it may not create its desired effect until sometime after the mining agents have departed. Although able to discriminate between target types, mines are unable to determine the nationality of a target. Unless sterilizers or self-destruct features are incorporated, the mine continues to be effective until swept or otherwise neutralized.

Note: A mine sterilizer is a countermeasure device designed to make a mine harmless after a preset number of days.

(2) When used, mines have inflicted disproportionate casualties compared with the mine emplacement effort. The collateral effects of mining operations, such as the diversion of shipping, the exposure of ships to other weapon systems, and the cost of MCM efforts, can have a major impact on war aims.

(3) The design of a naval minefield, and the type and number of mines to be used, depends on the field's purpose, expected adversary traffic, geographical location, amount of countermeasures to which it will be subjected, and the mining platforms to be used. Clever minefield design enables mining forces to achieve their objectives without excessive mining effort. Although neutralizing a single mine can prove easy, an entire minefield is considered to be the real challenge.

b. Types of Minefields.
Naval minefields can be characterized by their purpose and where they are laid, as follows:

(1) Offensive minefield: a minefield laid in enemy territorial water or waters under enemy control.

(2) Defensive minefield: a minefield laid in international waters or international straits with the declared intention of controlling shipping in defense of sea communications.

(3) Protective minefield: a minefield laid in friendly territorial waters to protect ports, harbors, anchorages, coasts, and coastal routes.

c. Mine Classification.
Naval mines are typically classified in one of three ways:

(1) Final position in the water. Discussed in follow-on paragraphs.

(2) Method of actuation. This includes contact, magnetic, acoustic, seismic, and pressure.

(3) Method of delivery. This includes air, surface, and submarine.

d. **Final Position in the Water.** When classified according to the position they assume in the water after placement, mines fall into three primary categories:

(1) Bottom mines.

(2) Moored mines.

(3) Moving mines.

Note: In US usage, the term "bottom mine" is always used, and the term "ground mine" should be avoided. In Allied usage, while "bottom mine" is the preferred usage, the term "ground mine" is still used in some contexts.

e. **Bottom Mines**

(1) Bottom mines are non-buoyant weapons. When planted, the mine case is in contact with the seabed and is held in place by its own weight. In areas with a soft bottom they may be completely or partially embedded. Such mines are referred to as buried mines. A mine that is resting on the bottom (unburied or partially buried) may also be referred to as a proud mine.

(2) There are two special categories of bottom mines that react differently from other bottom mines when they are initially emplaced, but they become similar once they have reached their final plant position:

(a) A moving bottom mine is a collective description for those designed to move along the bottom after being planted, but before becoming armed.

(b) A self-propelled mine is fitted with propulsion equipment, such as a torpedo, that is used to propel it to an intended final position. For example, a submarine could fire a self-propelled mine from a standoff point that is outside of the intended minefield location, and the mine would then propel itself to the desired location.

f. **Moored Mines**

(1) Moored mines have a buoyant case set at a certain depth beneath the surface. The mine is held in place above the seabed by means of a cable or chain that is attached to an anchor. The mines are frequently fitted with a self-destruct device that will cause them to flood and sink if separated from the anchor. Mines that separate from their anchors and rise to the surface are known as floaters. These may continue to float until they are struck and detonated, or they may deteriorate from their exposure to the seawater. Moored mines are designed for deep water, for use against both submarines and surface ships. The length and weight of the mooring cable and the mine case crush-depth will limit the maximum water depth in which they may be emplaced.

(2) A major disadvantage of moored mines is that the mooring cable can be cut with mechanical sweep apparatus. When this occurs, the case floats to the surface and must be avoided or destroyed. Another disadvantage is that they can be affected by current and tidal variations that cause the case to dip below its intended depth and change the angle for intended operation, thereby reducing its effectiveness against a surface target.

(3) There are two special types of moored mines that contain propulsion systems that enable them to quickly reach the intended target:

(a) Homing or guided mines are self-propelled moored mines that use guidance equipment to home onto a target once the target has been detected.

(b) A rising mine is a self-propelled or buoyant moored mine that releases from its mooring and rises to detonate on contact with (or proximity to) a target. It does not incorporate a homing device to guide it to the target, but contains logic circuitry that enables it to calculate an estimated target location.

g. **Moving Mines.** Moving mines are classified as either drifting or oscillating mines.

(1) **Drifting Mines**

(a) This is a mine that is buoyant or neutrally buoyant, but does not have an anchor or any other device to maintain it in a fixed position. It is free to move under the influence of wind, tide, or current. It may float at the water's surface or may be kept at a set depth beneath the surface by a depth-controlling hydrostatic device. It may be attached to a small piece of flotsam or other innocent-looking object, or even to another drifting mine. Two or more may be tethered together to increase the probability of striking a ship.

(b) Although banned from international waters by the 1907 Hague Treaty, these mines have been used on occasion. A drifting mine is classified differently from a moored mine that has become a floater, as a floater was designed to be anchored, while a drifter was designed to float freely with the tides and currents.

(c) The principal advantage of drifting mines is that their use is independent of bottom depth. The major drawback is that they scatter and may imperil friendly shipping. Consequently, drifters are usually fitted with devices designed to sink them after a short life span. As such, the most useful application has been in tactical situations in which they are placed in the path of an adversary to cause a delay or diversion.

(2) **Oscillating Mines**

(a) This is a drifting mine that regulates its depth by means of a hydrostatic control mechanism.

(b) The hydrostatic control mechanism causes it to oscillate at or near a preset water depth, which permits the mining of waters that are too deep for bottom or moored mines.

2. United States and Allied Mine Emplacement Assets

a. Mines reach their maximum effectiveness only when they are accurately positioned in time to be armed and ready for the transit of the first target ship. This requirement places the burden on operational forces to employ delivery vehicles with acceptable capabilities. As previously stated, mines may be delivered by aircraft, submarine, or surface craft. Selection depends on the various environmental and operational factors associated with each situation. The factors to be considered include:

(1) Type of minefield (defensive, offensive, or protective).

(2) Number and type of mines to be delivered.

(3) Number of sorties required.

(4) Defensive capabilities in area, attrition rate expected for delivery vehicles, and the need for standoff delivery systems.

(5) Environmental characteristics, such as water depth and bottom composition.

(6) Required accuracy in delivery.

(7) Logistics for coordinating stockpiled mines and delivery system.

b. **US Mine Inventory.** The US mine inventory consists of a variety of air- and submarine-delivered, influence-actuated mines. Sizes vary and include 500 to 2,000 pounds. The US mining program is designed to support offensive, defensive, and protective mining operations. Detailed discussion of these systems can be found in NTTP 3-15.1, *Maritime Mining*.

c. **Air Delivery.** Aircraft are the most suitable delivery vehicles for most offensive mining operations. In general, any aircraft capable of carrying bombs can carry a similar load of sea mines of the same weight class. There are some constraints and limitations imposed by matching suspension lugs on some mines to certain bomb racks, the shape and dimensional changes of some mines brought about by the addition of flight gear or fins, and the high drag and buffeting characteristics of mines carried on external stations. Several incompatibilities can be corrected with existing adapters and modification kits, but the performance limitations imposed on high-speed aircraft are also factors. Range, weather conditions, auxiliary equipment, and armament must be considered, as each can affect the maximum permissible load aboard the aircraft. The tactical manual of the individual aircraft is the final authority on mine carriage.

(1) **Advantages of Air Delivery.** There are a number of advantages associated with aerial delivery:

(a) Aircraft can penetrate areas inaccessible to ships and submarines and can replenish existing fields without danger from previously emplaced sea mines.

(b) Aircraft have a faster reaction time than surface ships or submarines.

(c) Aircraft are generally more readily available and can typically complete their mining mission quickly.

(d) Aircraft can carry a wide variety of naval mines.

(2) **Disadvantages of Air Delivery.** There are a number of disadvantages associated with air delivery, but for offensive scenarios, many of these can be overcome through proper planning.

(a) The payload-per-sortie is relatively small except for large, bomber aircraft. However, this disadvantage can be overcome by the ability to rapidly execute multiple sorties.

(b) Mine emplacement accuracy of aircraft is lower than for a surface ship but is adequate for offensive mining.

(c) Many aircraft types can be restricted by weather conditions.

(d) The range of aircraft is more restricted than that of surface ships or submarines.

(e) In general, aircraft deploy mines in a less clandestine manner than submarines (but more so than surface ships).

(f) Aircraft are vulnerable to enemy defenses, especially if the area to be mined is within the envelope of an enemy integrated air defense system.

(3) **Helicopter Delivery.** It is possible to deliver sea mines by helicopter, but such use is inefficient due to limited range and carrying capacity.

d. **Submarine Delivery.** Submarines are most effective in areas that are too well protected for surface or aircraft delivery. Normally, they will be used in offensive fields, but may be used to emplace defensive fields as well. This can take place day or night, surfaced or submerged. The availability of the Submarine-Launched Mobile Mine enhances the submarine capability.

(1) **Advantages of Submarine Delivery.** The advantages of submarine-delivered mines are:

(a) The clandestine nature of submarine delivery.

(b) Mission radius.

(c) Unrestricted by weather conditions.

(2) **Disadvantages of Submarine Delivery.** The disadvantages of submarine-delivered mines are:

(a) Limited payloads and weapons mix.

(b) Slow reaction time (i.e., if not loaded with mines for a contingency, submarine must return to a port for loading of naval mines).

(c) Slow transit speed when compared with aircraft delivery.

(d) Submarine availability with respect to competing mission requirements.

(e) Delay incurred in reconfiguring mines to fit a torpedo tube.

(f) Cannot replenish existing fields without danger from previously laid sea mines.

e. **Surface Delivery.** This is the preferred method for protective and defensive minefields where transit distances are limited and the area to be mined is benign. Any surface ship can be configured to emplace sea mines by hoisting or rolling them over the side or by using temporarily installed mine rails or tracks. Although mine emplacing ships of various types appeared on the Navy roster for about 60 years, there are no active surface ships in service today. However, should an operational requirement develop, this capability could be provided by crafting appendages and then engineering them to fit available ships. Suitable conversion of cargo ships is also an option. Some allies do have a surface mine emplacement capability.

(1) **Advantages of Surface Delivery**

(a) Able to carry a larger payload than aircraft or submarine mine emplacers.

(b) Surface assets have the ability to position mines more accurately than the other delivery assets.

(2) **Disadvantages of Surface Delivery**

(a) Surface ships have a slow reaction time and are not suitable when time is critical.

(b) Surface mine emplacement is not covert.

(c) They are vulnerable to attack, so they are not effective offensively.

(d) Surface ships are unable to replenish existing minefields.

3. **Additional Information**

Additional information on naval maritime MW capabilities can be found in the NWP 3-15, *Naval Mine Warfare*, series of publications, or by contacting Commander, NMAWC.

APPENDIX E
MARITIME MINE WARFARE AND MINE COUNTERMEASURES ORGANIZATION AND CAPABILITIES

1. Maritime Mine Warfare Force Organization

The Commander, USFF, and COMUSPACFLT are the administrative and operational commanders for the maritime MW forces. When other fleet commanders require maritime MW support, forces are provided through the numbered fleet commanders, with NMAWC coordination. Commander, USFF, and COMUSPACFLT normally exercise operational control over Navy Munitions Command (NMC) units—deployable mine assembly teams which are administratively consolidated with larger NMC detachments. These NMC units are directed by Commander, Mobile Mine Assembly Group, in response to mine-build orders generated by the NMAWC MW staff or the designated MIWC. The respective type commanders are responsible for maritime MW force readiness, and NMAWC, as the USN principal maritime MW advisor and Warfare Center of Excellence, is responsible for the integrated training, tactics, and interoperability of the maritime MW forces. These forces are required to be prepared to deploy on short notice to meet the CCDR's operational requirements. NMAWC maintains a deployable, scalable maritime MW staff to support fleet or combatant command staffs and provides technical advice to NATO and allied countries. Additionally, the USN maintains deployable tactical MCMRONs that report to NMAWC or other designated commander. These MCMRONs are operational staffs that exist to exercise tactical C2 of specified MCM forces (air, surface, and underwater).

a. **Command Relationships and Mission-Related Terminology.** The following command relationships are defined by joint doctrine, but are presented here for clarification as they relate to maritime MW-MCM (mining forces are considered strike warfare assets and are not discussed here). Assigned MCM units are placed within a command organization on a relatively permanent basis. An MCM 1 Class ship that deploys as part of an MCM task unit and a landing craft air cushion control ship (LCS) that is organized in an MCM task unit are examples of assigned MCM units.

(1) **Attached.** MCM units are temporarily placed within a command organization for short duration and specific operation. An MCM 1 Class ship or MW-configured LCS operating within a strike group to protect maneuver space are examples of an attached MCM unit.

(2) **Supporting.** MCM units that operate in general, mutual, direct, or close augmentation of a supported force, but remain assigned or attached to the supporting force commander.

b. **MCM Force Response Categories.** Current and future MCM forces fall into three categories based on response capability:

(1) **Immediate Response Force.** Immediate response forces are MCM forces in theater and in close proximity available for countering imminent threats and protecting

maneuver space. Immediate response forces are structured to provide MCM coverage rates that permit freedom of maneuver with minimal delay.

(2) **Rapid Response Force.** Rapid response forces are MCM contingency forces that can quickly arrive in theater. They consist of continental US (CONUS)-based, rapidly deployable forces and in-theater, forward-deployed naval forces, available to commence operations within 96 hours. The rapid response forces can augment immediate response forces for direct support to a strike group operation or provide theater mission support in advance of approaching forces.

(3) **Follow-On Force.** Follow-on forces are MCM forces that are time-phased to arrive in theater after combat operations commence. Follow-on forces execute large-scale MCM campaigns to expand the battlespace initially cleared by rapid response forces and conduct post-hostility mine clearance. These forces include CONUS-based AMCM and EOD forces not employed in the rapid response force and CONUS-based SMCM ships, which can self-deploy or be heavy-lifted into theater.

c. **US Mine Countermeasures Assets.** This section describes resources of the current USN MCM triad of forces, consisting of AMCM, SMCM, and UMCM systems and platforms. In most MCM operations, the US approach is to employ the triad working in concert. Each functional component of the triad offers complementary capabilities in MCM. The following paragraphs briefly describe US systems and platforms in service and planned.

(1) **AMCM.** This section describes the general capabilities of AMCM helicopters and their systems. Additional information on AMCM functions and capabilities are contained in NTTP 3-15.22, *Airborne Mine Countermeasures Operations*. The AMCM force consists of two squadrons of MH-53E helicopters, HM-14 and HM-15, and the AMCM Weapon Systems Training School. The operational squadrons are organized and trained for rapid deployment, and can be largely self-sustaining when operating in detachments from a large deck amphibious ship or a shore site. Principal capabilities of the aircraft include sonar minehunting/bottom mapping, with laser bottom mine identification; mechanical minesweeping; influence minesweeping; precision navigation; environmental reconnaissance. Typically, AMCM helicopters can carry and employ one MCM system at a time. The decision on which system to employ must be made well before the mission in order to configure the aircraft before flight.

(a) **MH-53E Helicopter.** The AMCM helicopter is the MH-53E Sea Dragon, a three-engine heavy-lift helicopter. Discussion of maximum and operational lift limitations can be found in Naval Air Training and Operating Procedures Standardization (NATOPS) Flight Manual A1-H53ME-NFM-000, *Navy Model MH-53E Helicopters*. The aircraft can fly for approximately four hours, assuming that environmental conditions do not restrict full-capacity fueling. More specific discussion of endurance and other limitations can also be found in NATOPS.

(b) **AMCM Systems.** The major equipment used by the current AMCM systems includes mechanical and influence (acoustic, magnetic, and combination) minesweeping equipment and minehunting sonar. The systems are modular to permit installation and removal.

(2) **Surface Mine Countermeasures.** The surface element of the MCM triad is the AVENGER (MCM 1) Class, which has the capability to hunt and sweep moored and bottom mines. MCM 1 Class vessels have minehunting and neutralization capabilities, and can conduct mechanical, influence, and combination minesweeping. Their hulls are constructed of wood with a laminated glass reinforced plastic outer shell to reduce magnetic signature. Propulsion is primarily diesel engines driving twin shafts, with backup electric light load propulsion motors powered by a marine minesweeping gas turbine generator for reduced acoustic signature. The gas turbine generator can also power a bow thruster, for station-keeping and low-speed maneuvering, or the magnetic influence sweeping equipment. These vessels participate in coordinated operations with amphibious and other supported forces, conduct independent operations, and participate in integrated MCM operations. While these vessels can operate for extended periods of time, their transit speed is slow, and therefore they are unable to deploy rapidly in support of contingency operations. They are often deployed by heavy-lift shipping, and availability of such assets must be considered. Some MCM 1 Class ships are permanently forward deployed to alleviate this circumstance. MCM equipment used aboard the MCM 1 Class includes mechanical and influence (acoustic, magnetic, and combination) minesweeping gear, a hull-mounted variable depth high-frequency sonar, and a tethered pilotable minehunting unmanned underwater vessel (UUV) capable of identifying and neutralizing naval mines. Additional information on SMCM functions and capabilities is contained in NTTP 3-15.21, *Surface Mine Countermeasures (SMCM) Operations*. Principal SMCM operational capabilities are:

(a) Minehunting sonar.

(b) Remotely operated vehicle mine neutralization.

(c) Mechanical moored minesweeping.

(d) Influence minesweeping.

(e) Combination sweeping (mechanical-acoustic and magnetic-acoustic).

(f) Support of EOD operations to neutralize, destroy, and exploit mines.

(g) Magnetic silencing.

(h) Precision navigation.

(i) Environmental measuring.

(j) Buoying equipment.

(k) Nonferrous design throughout to reduce magnetic signature.

(l) Propulsion designed to reduce acoustic signature.

(3) **UMCM.** This section describes the general capabilities of UMCM assets and their systems. Additional information on UMCM functions and capabilities contained in NTTP 3-15.23, *Underwater Mine Countermeasures (UMCM)*.

(a) **EOD.** EOD platoons and combat systems provide mine detection, classification, identification, neutralization, and exploitation capability in confined areas, including inland waterways. Strike group EOD platoons are multi-mission assets that perform UMCM operations to reacquire, identify, and neutralize floating, moored, and bottom mines.

(b) **EOD MCM Platoons.** EOD MCM platoons are functionally specialized to locate, identify, neutralize, recover, exploit, and dispose of ordnance in the UMCM environment. EOD MCM platoons normally work in conjunction with marine mammal systems detachments, in support of SMCM and AMCM platforms. They are capable of independent MCM operations.

(c) **EOD Mobile Unit One (EODMU)-1.** EODMU-1 executes MCM from over-the-horizon to the seaward edge of the SZ (normally the 10-foot depth contour). The team conducts low-visible exploration and reconnaissance to locate and prepare sea mines and obstacles for neutralization, in support of amphibious assaults. EODMU-1 also provides hydrographic reconnaissance reports to the MIWC to support MCM missions.

(d) **Navy Oceanographic Mine Warfare Center (NOMWC).** NOMWC provides ongoing support for the Navy's MW forces to neutralize threats and to allow for assured access of maritime assets. It also provides the Navy's MW operators with access to products and services of the Naval Oceanographic Office. The NOMWC UUV platoon provides operational employment of UUVs for oceanographic survey in support of MW. The platoon also supports test and evaluation of UUV systems in support of the MW oceanographic mission. NOMWC reports to the Naval Oceanography Operations Command, a subordinate of the Commander, Naval Meteorology and Oceanography Command, which directs all of the Navy's meteorology and oceanography programs. All are located at Stennis, Mississippi.

APPENDIX F
HUMANITARIAN MINE ACTION

"I think we do agree on one central goal, and that is the need to end the threat that land mines pose to civilians. The best way to do that is to proceed full speed ahead with the job of pulling mines from the soil like the noxious weeds that they are. I am proud that the United States is far and away the world leader in mine removal programs."

Madeleine K. Albright
Secretary of State, 8 April 1999

1. Evolution of United States Humanitarian Mine Action

a. Modern US HMA began in 1986, when US Army special forces teams in southern Honduras trained Honduran Army engineers to clear land mines from agricultural land north of the Nicaraguan border.

b. In 1988, a United States Agency for International Development team traveled to Afghanistan to assess the land mine situation following the Soviet occupation. The National Security Council officially established the US Humanitarian Demining Program in 1993.

c. The current Department of Defense (DOD) Humanitarian Mine Action Program began in 1995, under the Assistant Secretary of Defense (Special Operations/Low-Intensity Conflict and Interdependent Capabilities) (ASD[SO/LIC&IC]), the DOD office most closely associated with US special operations forces (SOF).

d. US Army special forces, MISO teams, CA officers, and other SOF and DOD elements began working toward the goal of assisting mine-affected nations in developing self-sustaining indigenous military action programs.

e. In June 1998, the Department of State (DOS) established the Office of Humanitarian Demining Programs in its Bureau of Political-Military Affairs to coordinate overall United States Government (USG) HMA work. An interagency working group (IWG) was established to facilitate HMA cooperation within the USG.

2. Humanitarian Mine Action Program

a. **Mission.** The USG HMA program assists countries in relieving the suffering of the adverse effects of uncleared land mines while promoting US interests. To achieve these goals, the USG balances various political, military, economic, and technological capabilities with available resources.

b. The DOD program is directly supervised by the GCCs and is a critical component of the overall USG program. DOD's program concentrates on training HNs in the procedures of land mine clearance, mine awareness, and victims' assistance, as well as the development of leadership and organizational skills necessary to sustain the programs after US military trainers have redeployed. This approach provides unique training and readiness-enhancing benefits to US SOFs while advancing GCCs' theater security cooperation strategies. The program is authorized by Title 10, US Code (USC), Section 401. In 2004, DOD support for HMA expanded to include conventional forces.

c. Title 10, USC, Section 401(a)(4), prohibits members of the Armed Forces of the United States from engaging in the physical detection, lifting, or destroying of land mines (unless the member does so for the concurrent purpose of supporting a US military operation). Additionally, members of the Armed Forces of the United States shall not provide such humanitarian and civic assistance as part of a military operation that does not involve the armed forces. This humanitarian and civic assistance, per Title 10, USC, Section 401(e)(5), includes "detection and clearance of land mines and other ERW, including activities relating to the furnishing of education, training, and technical assistance with respect to the detection and clearance of land mines and other explosive remnants of war."

d. Significant benefits accrue to DOD: the program provides access to geographical areas otherwise not easily accessible by US forces. It also contributes to unit and individual readiness by providing unique in-country training opportunities that cannot be duplicated in the United States. For example, US military forces hone critical wartime, civil-military, language, cultural, and foreign internal defense skills.

3. Oversight and Policy Direction

a. The US DOS sets policy and provides overall direction for US HMA. Within DOS, the Office of Humanitarian Demining Programs serves as the lead organization in coordinating US HMA activities worldwide. The office develops and implements country-specific HDM programs and oversees the interagency strategic planning and policy development processes supporting US global military activities. The DOS Office of Humanitarian Demining Programs directly supports the work of the IWG on HDM. Within DOS, HDM oversight is located within the Office of Weapons Removal and Abatement, Bureau of Political-Military Affairs.

b. **US Policy and DOD Role in HMA.** DOS makes several important points regarding DOD HMA work:

(1) The USG provides HMA assistance to many countries throughout the world to relieve human suffering from the dangers of land mines, to promote regional peace and stability and to promote US foreign policy and national security goals. A collateral benefit to the program is the enhancement of operational readiness skills of participating US forces.

(2) Within the overall USG HMA program, DOD provides training to foreign nations in mine clearance operations, mine awareness education and information campaigns, assistance in the establishment of HMA centers, emergency medical care, and leadership and management skills needed to successfully conduct a national-level HMA program.

(3) When called upon for mine-action training, the ultimate goal of DOD participation is to develop a self-sustaining, indigenous demining capability within each

recipient country. SOF normally conduct HMA training, using the "train-the-trainer" concept, with augmentation from EOD and engineer personnel, as needed.

(4) The GCCs execute the HMA program, providing them an excellent military-to-military engagement opportunity. DOD participation in HMA programs allows the GCCs to work closely with country teams to show mine-affected countries how military forces can support the civilian population.

(5) By participating in these activities, the combatant commands and the country teams demonstrate the US commitment to provide direct, bilateral humanitarian assistance, relieve suffering, improve the socio-economic environment, promote regional stability, and support democratic ideals.

(6) **DOD Roles.** Generally, DOD funds an HMA program's start-up costs, and DOS provides subsequent funds to procure the necessary equipment for mine-affected countries to conduct mine clearance operations. Additional funds support DOD-sponsored demining technology research and development. DOD roles can be summarized as follows:

(a) In coordination with the Defense Security Cooperation Agency (DSCA) allocates DOD funds for the DOD element of the USG HDM program.

(b) Assists host countries in the establishment of HDM organizations.

(c) Coordinates US HDM training with Fort Leonard Wood Humanitarian Demining Training Center.

(7) The components of the DOD humanitarian HMA program are:

(a) Mine awareness education.

(b) Mine action center development.

(c) Civil-military cooperation.

(d) Victim assistance.

(e) HMA training—or train-the-trainer—the core of the program. More than 4,000 indigenous trainers have benefited from this core program.

4. The Interagency Working Group on Humanitarian Demining

An IWG on land mines and demining has been established at the request of the National Security Council. The announcement of the Demining 2010 Initiative in October 1997 created a separate responsibility, generating increased international coordination and contributions for HDM, complementary to the mandate of this IWG.

a. **IWG Members.** IWG members include:

(1) National Security Council.

(2) DOS (chairman).

(3) DOD (vice chairman).

(4) United States Agency for International Development.

(5) Designated members of the intelligence community.

b. **Office of the Assistant Secretary of Defense for International Security Affairs, DSCA, Office of Humanitarian Assistance, Disaster Relief and Mine Action.**

(1) Acts as DOD's lead HDM agency by exercising overall responsibility, corporate level policy, planning, and oversight for DOD HDM programs conducted pursuant to Title 10, USC, Section 401. The HMA program assists countries that are experiencing the adverse affects of uncleared land mines and other ERW. The program is directly managed by the CCDRs and contributes to unit and individual readiness by providing unique in-country training opportunities that cannot be duplicated in the US.

(2) Provides the vice chairman of the IWG and cochairs the sub-IWG.

(3) Develops and implements DOD HDM activities based on applicable presidential policy guidance coordinated through the IWG.

(4) Coordinates and authorizes funding for DOD HDM operations and related activities.

(5) Oversees the CCDRs' operational mine action, humanitarian, and civic assistance programs.

c. **DSCA**

(1) Coordinates and monitors execution of DOD HDM training operations and related program activities. In coordination with ASD(SO/LIC&IC), plans, programs, budgets for, and allocates budget authority from the Overseas, Humanitarian, Disaster, and Civic Aid appropriation to support the DOD HDM program.

(2) Assists the Joint Chiefs of Staff, US Special Operations Command, GCCs, host countries, and other organizations in planning for, establishing, and executing HMA programs.

(3) Coordinates with DOS on security assistance policy, budget planning, and execution issues for demining activities.

(4) Manages host countries' foreign military financing and specified nonproliferation, antiterrorism, demining, and related projects accounts.

(5) Sells defense articles and services, through the Foreign Military Sales program, to host countries for support of HMA programs.

d. **CJCS:**

(1) The Joint Staff/J-3 Operations Directorate is the office of primary responsibility for HMA activities.

(2) Coordinates requested HMA operations and force allocation with GCCs and supporting CCDRs.

(3) Provides HMA mission taskings, guidance, specific instructions, and operational control authority to the GCCs.

(4) Ensures that plans developed by CCDRs include, at minimum, the number of training deployments anticipated for each mine-affected country in the area of responsibility and time-phasing and milestones for each operation. Any subsequent training missions or assessments required should also be included, as well as other factors (such as projected resource requirements) that will be necessary to plan for and execute the proposed mission.

(5) Provides oversight Armed Forces of the United States training programs outside CONUS with partner nations.

e. **GCC:**

(1) Plans, manages, and conducts HDM training operations within the GCC's area of responsibility.

(2) Recommends and prioritizes theater HDM program recommendations through the Joint Staff to Office of the Assistant Secretary of Defense, DSCA, and the IWG.

(3) Executes DOD-funded HDM programs in host countries.

(4) Coordinates US participation in specified multilateral HDM operations (e.g., those sponsored by the Organization of American States).

(5) Conducts assessment for HDM programs and HMA technologies.

(6) Formulates polices for HMA training within DOD, in coordination with Deputy Assistant Secretary for Stability Operations, Special Operations and Low-Intensity Conflict.

5. Interagency Humanitarian Demining Strategic Plan

The plan, written by DOS, defines roles of the various USG agencies. In recent years, changing roles and responsibilities among USG agencies participating in the US Humanitarian Demining Program and the rapid expansion of the program have necessitated updates in the Interagency Humanitarian Demining Strategic Plan. These revisions are based on experiences and lessons learned over the last few years on HDM efforts. The strategic plan is designed to accelerate and make more effective USG efforts to make mine-affected countries around the world mine-safe. A complete summary of the US Demining Policy:

USG Interagency Humanitarian Demining Strategic Plan can be found at the DOS Web site at www.state.gov/t/pm/wra.

6. Additional Information

Additional and up-to-date information on HDM can be found by contacting:

a. **Humanitarian Demining Contact Information**

Mailing address:
US DOD
Humanitarian Demining Training Center
ATTN: ATSE-HAMA-HDM
Bldg 5415, FLW Hwy 38
Ft. Leonard Wood, MO 65473
Map and driving directions on student information page of Web site.

Telephone:
Commercial: 573-563-6199
DSN: 676-6199
Fax: 573-563-5051
E-mail: atsedotHDM@wood.army.mil
Ft. Leonard Wood home page: www.wood.army.mil

b. **DSCA Contact Information**

Mailing address:
DSCA
Office of Humanitarian Assistance and Mine Action
1111 Jefferson Davis Highway
Suite #402
Arlington, VA 22202

Telephone:
Commercial: 703-601-3657
Fax: 703-602-0075
E-mail: LPA-WEB@dsca.mil
DSCA HA home page: http://www.dsca.osd.mil/programs/HA/HA.htm

APPENDIX G
REFERENCES

The development of JP 3-15 is based upon the following primary references.

1. Public Laws

    a. Title 10, USC.

    b. Title 13, USC.

    c. Title 14, USC.

2. Strategic Guidance and Policy

    a. National Military Strategy of the United States of America.

    b. Memorandum of Agreement (MOA) Between the Department of Defense and the Department of Homeland Security on the Use of the US Coast Guard Capabilities and Resources in Support of the National Military Strategy.

3. Department of Defense Publications

    DOD Directive 5101.2, *DOD Executive Agent for Construction/Barrier Material.*

4. Chairman of the Joint Chiefs of Staff Publications

    a. CJCS Instruction 3150.25D, *Joint Lessons Learned Program.*

    b. CJCS Instruction 3207.01B, *Military Support to Humanitarian Mine Action.*

    c. CJCS Manual 3122.03C, *Joint Operation Planning and Execution System, Vol. II, Planning Formats.*

    d. CJCS Manual 6120.05, *Manual for Tactical Command and Control Planning Guidance for Joint Operations—Joint Interface Operational Procedures for Message Text Formats.*

    e. JP 1, *Doctrine for the Armed Forces of the United States.*

    f. JP 2-0, *Joint Intelligence.*

    g. JP 2-01.3, *Joint Intelligence Preparation of the Operational Environment.*

    h. JP 2-03, *Geospatial Intelligence Support to Joint Operations.*

    i. JP 3-0, *Joint Operations.*

    j. JP 3-02, *Amphibious Operations.*

k. JP 3-05.1, *Joint Special Operations Task Force Operations.*

l. JP 3-06, *Joint Urban Operations.*

m. JP 3-13, *Information Operations.*

n. JP 3-18, *Joint Forcible Entry Operations.*

o. JP 3-34, *Joint Engineer Operations.*

p. JP 3-59, *Meteorological and Oceanographic Operations.*

5. Multi-Service Publications

a. FM 3-90.119, MCIP 3-17.01, *Combined Arms Improvised Explosive Device Defeat Operations.*

b. FM 3-100.38, MCRP 3-17.2B, NTTP 3-02.4.1, AFTTP(I) 3-2.12, *Multi-Service Tactics, Techniques, and Procedures for Unexploded Explosive Ordnance Operations.*

c. FM 21-16, MCRP 3-17.2A, *Unexploded Ordnance (UXO) Procedures.*

d. FM 3-34.300/MCWP 17.6, *Survivability Operations.*

e. FM 3-34.210, MCRP 3-17.2D, *Explosive Hazards Operations.*

f. FM 3-34-214, MCRP 3-17.7L, *Explosives and Demolitions.*

g. FM 3-90.4, MCWP 3-17.8, *Combined Arms Mobility Operations.*

h. FM 3-90.119/MCIP 3-17.01, *Combined Arms Improvised Explosive Device Defeat Operations.*

g. FM 4-30.16/MCRP 3-17.2C/NTTP 3-02.5/AFTTP(I) 3-2.32, *Multi-Service Tactics, Techniques, and Procedures for Explosive Ordnance Disposal in a Joint Environment.*

h. MCRP 3-31.2A/NTTP 3-15.24, *Mine Countermeasures in Support of Amphibious Operations.*

i. MCWP 5-12.1, NWP 1-14M, Commandant of the Coast Guard Publication P5800.7A, *The Commander's Handbook on the Law of Naval Operations.*

6. US Army Publications

a. FM 3-06.11, *Combined Arms Operations in Urban Terrain.*

b. FM 3-34, *Engineer Operations.*

c. FM 3-34.22, *Engineer Operations—Brigade Combat Team and Below.*

d. FM 3-90.6, *The Brigade Combat Team.*

e. FM 3-90.61, *Brigade Special Troops Battalion.*

f. FM 90-7, *Combined Arms Obstacle Integration.*

g. ATTP 3-34.22, *Engineer Operations—Brigade Combat Team and Below.*

7. US Navy Publications

a. NWP 3-02.4, *Explosive Ordnance Disposal.*

b. NWP 3-05, *Naval Special Warfare.*

c. NWP 3-15, *Naval Mine Warfare.*

8. US Marine Corps Publications

a. MCWP 3-17.3, *MAGTF Breaching Operations.*

b. Marine Tactical Publication (MTP) 6, Vol. II, *Naval Mine Countermeasures Operations Planning and Evaluation.*

c. MTP 24, Vol. I, *Naval Mine Countermeasures Tactics and Execution.*

9. Other Publications

a. Variable Message Format (VMF) Message Number K05.16, *Land Minefield Laying Report, TIDP-TE, Vol. III, Annex A.*

b. TC 20-32-3, *Foreign Mine Handbook (Balkan States).*

c. TC 20-32-4, *Foreign Mine Handbook (Asia).*

d. TC 20-32-5, *Commander's Reference Guide: Land Mine and Explosive Hazards (Iraq).*

e. Allied Tactical Publication (ATP) 1 (C), *Vol. I, Allied Maritime Tactical Instructions.*

f. ATP 1 (C), *Vol. II, Allied Maritime Tactical Instructions and Procedures.*

g. Allied Procedural Publication-4, *Allied Formatted and Standard Messages.*

h. ATP 6C (Navy) (Air), *Volume I, Allied Doctrine of Mine Warfare, Policies, and Principles.*

i. ATP 24 (C) (Navy), *Tactical Instructions and Procedures for the Conduct of Mine Warfare Operations.*

j. Standardization Agreement (STANAG) 2036, *Land Minefield Laying, Marking, Recording, and Reporting Procedures.*

k. STANAG 2430, *Land Force Combat Engineer Messages, Reports, and Returns (AEngrP-2).*

l. STANAG 2485, *Countermine Operations in Land Warfare.*

m. United States Joint Forces Command Handbook, *Organizing for Improvised Explosive Device Defeat (IEDD) at the Operational Level.*

APPENDIX H
ADMINISTRATIVE INSTRUCTIONS

1. User Comments

Users in the field are highly encouraged to submit comments on this publication to: Joint Staff J-7, Deputy Director, Joint and Coalition Warfighting, Joint and Coalition Warfighting Center, ATTN: Joint Doctrine Support Division, 116 Lake View Parkway, Suffolk, VA 23435-2697. These comments should address content (accuracy, usefulness, consistency, and organization), writing, and appearance.

2. Authorship

The lead agent for this publication is the US Army. The Joint Staff doctrine sponsor for this publication is the Joint Staff Logistics Directorate (J-4).

3. Supersession

This publication supersedes JP 3-15, 26 April 2007, *Barriers, Obstacles, and Mine Warfare for Joint Operations*.

4. Change Recommendations

a. Recommendations for urgent changes to this publication should be submitted:

```
TO:     CSA WASHINGTON DC//DAMO-FDQ//
INFO:   JOINT STAFF WASHINGTON DC//J7-JEDD//
```

Routine changes should be submitted electronically to the Deputy Director, Joint and Coalition Warfighting, Joint and Coalition Warfighting Center, Joint Doctrine Support Division and info the lead agent and the Director for Joint Force Development, J-7/JEDD.

b. When a Joint Staff directorate submits a proposal to the CJCS that would change source document information reflected in this publication, that directorate will include a proposed change to this publication as an enclosure to its proposal. The Services and other organizations are requested to notify the Joint Staff J-7 when changes to source documents reflected in this publication are initiated.

5. Distribution of Publications

Local reproduction is authorized and access to unclassified publications is unrestricted. However, access to and reproduction authorization for classified JPs must be in accordance with DOD 5200.1-R, *Information Security Program*.

6. Distribution of Electronic Publications

a. Joint Staff J-7 will not print copies of JPs for distribution. Electronic versions are available on JDEIS at https://jdeis.js.mil (NIPRNET), and http://jdeis.js.smil.mil (SIPRNET), and on the JEL at http://www.dtic.mil/doctrine (NIPRNET).

b. Only approved JPs and joint test publications are releasable outside the CCMDs, Services, and Joint Staff. Release of any classified JP to foreign governments or foreign nationals must be requested through the local embassy (Defense Attaché Office) to DIA, Defense Foreign Liaison/IE-3, 200 MacDill Blvd., Joint Base Anacostia-Bolling, Washington, DC 20340-5100.

c. JEL CD-ROM. Upon request of a joint doctrine development community member, the Joint Staff J-7 will produce and deliver one CD-ROM with current JPs. This JEL CD-ROM will be updated not less than semi-annually and when received can be locally reproduced for use within the combatant commands and Services.

GLOSSARY
PART I—ABBREVIATIONS AND ACRONYMS

ACE   aviation combat element (MAGTF)
AFTTP(I)   Air Force tactics, techniques, and procedures (instruction)
AHD   antihandling device
AMC   Air Mobility Command
AMCM   airborne mine countermeasures
AOA   amphibious objective area
AP   antipersonnel
APL   antipersonnel land mine
ASD(SO/LIC&IC)   Assistant Secretary of Defense for Special Operations and
                     Low-Intensity Conflict and Interdependent Capabilities
ATF   amphibious task force
ATP   allied tactical publication
ATTP   Army tactics, techniques, and procedures
AVL   anti-vehicle land mine

BCT   brigade combat team

C2   command and control
CA   civil affairs
CATF   commander, amphibious task force
CBRN   chemical, biological, radiological, and nuclear
CCDR   combatant commander
CCW   1980 United Nations Convention on Conventional
                     Weapons
CEB   combat engineer battalion
CJCS   Chairman of the Joint Chiefs of Staff
CLF   commander, landing force
COA   course of action
COMUSPACFLT   Commander, United States Pacific Fleet
CONOPS   concept of operations
CONUS   continental United States
COP   common operational picture
CS   combat support
CTU   commander, task unit

DOD   Department of Defense
DOS   Department of State
DSCA   Defense Security Cooperation Agency

EH   explosive hazard
EHCC   explosive hazards coordination cell
EOD   explosive ordnance disposal
EODMU   explosive ordnance disposal mobile unit

ERT	engineer reconnaissance team
ERW	explosive remnants of war
ESB	engineer support battalion
FM	field manual (Army)
GCC	geographic combatant commander
GCE	ground combat element (MAGTF)
GEOINT	geospatial intelligence
GI&S	geospatial information and services
HBCT	heavy brigade combat team
HDM	humanitarian demining
HMA	humanitarian mine action
HN	host nation
IBCT	infantry brigade combat team
IED	improvised explosive device
IO	information operations
IPB	intelligence preparation of the battlespace
IWG	interagency working group
JEL	Joint Electronic Library
JFACC	joint force air component commander
JFC	joint force commander
JFMCC	joint force maritime component commander
JIPOE	joint intelligence preparation of the operational environment
JOPP	joint operation planning process
JP	joint publication
JTCB	joint targeting coordination board
K-Kill	catastrophic kill
LCE	logistics combat element (MAGTF)
LCS	landing craft air cushion control ship
LF	landing force
LOC	line of communications
LZ	landing zone
MAC	mobility assault company
MAGTF	Marine air-ground task force
MCIP	Marine Corps interim publication
MCM	mine countermeasures
MCMC	mine countermeasures commander
MCMREP	mine countermeasure report

MCMRON	mine countermeasures squadron
MCRP	Marine Corps reference publication
MCWP	Marine Corps warfighting publication
METT-T	mission, enemy, terrain and weather, troops and support available—time available
MIL-STD	military standard
MISO	military information support operations
MIWC	mine warfare commander
M-Kill	mobility kill
MP	military police (Army and Marine)
MPSRON	maritime pre-positioning ships squadron
MTP	Marine tactical publication
MW	mine warfare
NATO	North Atlantic Treaty Organization
NATOPS	Naval Air Training and Operating Procedures Standardization
NCC	Navy component commander
NMAWC	Naval Mine and Anti-Submarine Warfare Command
NMC	Navy Munitions Command
NOMWC	Navy Oceanographic Mine Warfare Center
NTTP	Navy tactics, techniques, and procedures
NWP	Navy warfare publication
OBSTINT	obstacle intelligence
OPLAN	operation plan
OPORD	operation order
OPTASK	operation task
RCT	regimental combat team
ROE	rules of engagement
ROK	Republic of Korea
SBCT	Stryker brigade combat team
SecDef	Secretary of Defense
SLOC	sea line of communications
SMCM	surface mine countermeasures
SOF	special operations forces
SOP	standard operating procedure
SPOTREP	spot report
STANAG	standardization agreement (NATO)
SZ	surf zone
TC	training circular
TTP	tactics, techniques, and procedures

UMCM	underwater mine countermeasures
UN	United Nations
UNCLOS	United Nations Convention on Law of the Sea
US	United States
USAF	United States Air Force
USC	United States Code
USCG	United States Coast Guard
USFF	United States Fleet Forces Command
USG	United States Government
USN	United States Navy
USNORTHCOM	United States Northern Command
USPACOM	United States Pacific Command
UUV	unmanned underwater vessel
UXO	unexploded explosive ordnance
WBIED	waterborne improvised explosive device
WMD	weapons of mass destruction

antitank mine. None. (Approved for removal from JP 1-02.)

anti-vehicle land mine. A mine designed to immobilize or destroy a vehicle. Also called **AVL.** (Approved for inclusion in JP 1-02.)

arming. As applied to explosives, weapons, and ammunition, the changing from a safe condition to a state of readiness for initiation. (Approved for incorporation into JP 1-02 with JP 3-15 as the source JP.)

barrier. A coordinated series of natural or man-made obstacles designed or employed to channel, direct, restrict, delay, or stop the movement of an opposing force and to impose additional losses in personnel, time, and equipment on the opposing force. (Approved for incorporation into JP 1-02.)

barrier, obstacle, and mine warfare plan. A comprehensive, coordinated plan that includes responsibilities; general location of unspecified and specific barriers, obstacles, and minefields; special instructions; limitations; coordination; and completion times; and may designate locations of obstacle zones or belts. (Approved for incorporation into JP 1-02.)

bottom mine. A mine with negative buoyancy which remains on the seabed. (JP 1-02. SOURCE: JP 3-15)

canalize. To restrict operations to a narrow zone by use of existing or reinforcing obstacles or by fire or bombing. (Approved for incorporation into JP 1-02 with JP 3-15 as the source JP.)

chemical horn. None. (Approved for removal from JP 1-02.)

clearing operation. An operation designed to clear or neutralize all mines and obstacles from a route or area. (JP 1-02. SOURCE: JP 3-15)

command detonated mine. None. (Approved for removal from JP 1-02.)

contact mine. A mine detonated by physical contact. (Approved for incorporation into JP 1-02 with JP 3-15 as the source JP.)

conventional mines. Land mines, other than nuclear or chemical, that are not designed to self-destruct; are designed to be emplaced by hand or mechanical means; and can be buried or surface emplaced. (Approved for incorporation into JP 1-02.)

counterbattery fire. None. (Approved for removal from JP 1-02.)

creeping mine. None. (Approved for removal JP 1-02.)

defensive minefield. 1. In naval mine warfare, a minefield laid in international waters or international straits with the declared intention of controlling shipping in defense of sea communications. 2. In land mine warfare, a minefield laid in accordance with an established plan to prevent a penetration between positions and to strengthen the defense of the positions themselves. (Approved for incorporation into JP 1-02 with JP 3-15 as the source JP.)

degaussing. The process whereby a ship's magnetic field is reduced by the use of electromagnetic coils, permanent magnets, or other means. (Approved for incorporation into JP 1-02 with JP 3-15 as the source JP.)

denial measure. An action to hinder or deny the enemy the use of territory, personnel, or facilities to include destruction, removal, contamination, or erection of obstructions. (Approved for incorporation into JP 1-02.)

dip. None. (Approved for removal from JP 1-02.)

dormant. None. (Approved for removal from JP 1-02.)

enabling mine countermeasures. None. (Approved for removal from JP 1-02.)

exclusive economic zone. A maritime zone adjacent to the territorial sea that may not extend beyond 200 nautical miles from the baselines from which the breadth of the territorial sea is measured. Also called **EEZ.** (Approved for incorporation into JP 1-02)

explosive hazard. Any hazard containing an explosive component to include unexploded explosive ordnance (including land mines), booby traps (some booby traps are nonexplosive), improvised explosive devices (which are an improvised type of booby trap), captured enemy ammunition, and bulk explosives. Also called **EH.** (Approved for incorporation into JP 1-02.)

flame field expedients. Simple, handmade devices used to produce flame or illumination. Also called **FFE.** (JP 1-02. SOURCE: JP 3-15)

gap. None. (Approved for removal from JP 1-02.)

ground mine. None. (Approved for removal Upon approval of this revision, this term and its definition will be removed from JP 1-02.)

hasty breach. The creation of lanes through enemy minefields by expedient methods such as blasting with demolitions, pushing rollers or disabled vehicles through the minefields when the time factor does not permit detailed reconnaissance, deliberate breaching, or bypassing the obstacle. (Approved for replacement of "hasty breaching (land mine warfare)" in JP 1-02.)

Hertz-Horn. None. (Approved for removal from JP 1-02.)

humanitarian mine action. Activities that strive to reduce the social, economic, and environmental impact of land mines, unexploded ordnance and small arms ammunition—also characterized as explosive remnants of war. (JP 1-02. SOURCE: JP 3-15)

improvised mine. None. (Approved for removal from JP 1-02.)

influence mine. A mine actuated by the effect of a target on some physical condition in the vicinity of the mine or on radiations emanating from the mine. (JP 1-02. SOURCE: JP 3-15)

influence sweep. A sweep designed to produce an influence similar to that produced by a ship and thus actuate mines. (Approved for incorporation into JP 1-02 with JP 3-15 as the source JP.)

land mine warfare. None. (Approved for removal from JP 1-02.)

magnetic circuit. None. (Approved for removal from JP 1-02.)

magnetic mine. A mine that responds to the magnetic field of a target. (Approved for incorporation into JP 1-02.)

make safe. None. (Approved for removal from JP 1-02.)

mechanical sweep. In naval mine warfare, any sweep used with the object of physically contacting the mine or its appendages. (Approved for incorporation into JP 1-02 with JP 3-15 as the source JP.)

mine. 1. In land mine warfare, an explosive or other material, normally encased, designed to destroy or damage ground vehicles, boats, or aircraft, or designed to wound, kill, or otherwise incapacitate personnel and designed to be detonated by the action of its victim, by the passage of time, or by controlled means. 2. In naval mine warfare, an explosive device laid in the water with the intention of damaging or sinking ships or of deterring shipping from entering an area. (Approved for incorporation into JP 1-02.)

mineable waters. None. (Approved for removal from JP 1-02.)

mine-cluster. None. (Approved for removal from JP 1-02.)

mine countermeasures. All methods for preventing or reducing damage or danger from mines. Also called **MCM.** (JP 1-02. SOURCE JP 3-15)

mine disposal. None. (Approved for removal from JP 1-02.)

minefield. 1. In land warfare, an area of ground containing mines emplaced with or without a pattern. 2. In naval warfare, an area of water containing mines emplaced with or without a pattern. (Approved for incorporation into JP 1-02.)

minefield breaching. None. (Approved for removal from JP 1-02.)

minefield density. None. (Approved for removal from JP 1-02.)

minefield lane. None. (Approved for removal from JP 1-02.)

minefield marking. None. (Approved for removal from JP 1-02.)

minefield record. A complete written record of all pertinent information concerning a minefield, submitted on a standard form by the officer in charge of the emplacement operations. (Approved for incorporation into JP 1-02.)

minefield report. An oral, electronic, or written communication concerning mining activities (friendly or enemy) submitted in a standard format by the fastest secure means available. (JP 1-02. SOURCE: JP 3-15)

minehunting. Employment of sensor and neutralization systems, whether air, surface, or subsurface, to locate and dispose of individual mines in a known field, or to verify the presence or absence of mines in a given area. (Approved for incorporation into JP 1-02.)

minesweeping. The technique of clearing mines using either mechanical sweeping to remove, disturb, or otherwise neutralize the mine; explosive sweeping to cause sympathetic detonations, damage, or displace the mine; or influence sweeping to produce either the acoustic or magnetic influence required to detonate the mine. (Approved for incorporation into JP 1-02.)

mine warfare. The strategic, operational, and tactical use of mines and mine countermeasures either by emplacing mines to degrade the enemy's capabilities to wage land, air, and maritime warfare or by countering of enemy-emplaced mines to permit friendly maneuver or use of selected land or sea areas. Also called **MW.** (Approved for incorporation into JP 1-02.)

moored mine. A contact or influence-operated mine of positive buoyancy held below the surface by a mooring attached to a sinker or anchor on the bottom. (JP 1-02. SOURCE: JP 3-15)

networked munitions. Remotely controlled, interconnected, weapons system designed to provide rapidly emplaced ground-based countermobility and protection capability through scalable application of lethal and nonlethal means. (Approved for inclusion in JP 1-02.)

nuisance minefield. A minefield laid to delay and disorganize the enemy and to hinder the use of an area or route. (Approved for incorporation into JP 1-02 with JP 3-15 as the source JP.)

obstacle. Any natural or man-made obstruction designed or employed to disrupt, fix, turn, or block the movement of an opposing force, and to impose additional losses in personnel, time, and equipment on the opposing force. (Approved for incorporation into JP 1-02.)

obstacle belt. A brigade-level command and control measure, normally given graphically, to show where within an obstacle zone the ground tactical commander plans to limit friendly obstacle employment and focus the defense. (Approved for incorporation into JP 1-02.)

obstacle clearing. The total elimination or neutralization of obstacles. (Approved for incorporation into JP 1-02 with JP 3-15 as the source JP.)

obstacle intelligence. Those collection efforts to detect the presence of enemy and natural obstacles, determine their types and dimensions, and provide the necessary information to plan appropriate combined arms breaching, clearance, or bypass operations to negate the impact on the friendly scheme of maneuver. Also called **OBSTINT.** (Approved for incorporation into JP 1-02.)

obstacle restricted areas. A command and control measure used to limit the type or number of obstacles within an area. (JP 1-02. SOURCE: JP 3-15)

obstacle zone. A division-level command and control measure, normally done graphically, to designate specific land areas where lower echelons are allowed to employ tactical obstacles. (JP 1-02. SOURCE: JP 3-15)

offensive minefield. None. (Approved for removal from JP 1-02.)

operational control authority. The naval commander responsible within a specified geographical area for the naval control of all merchant shipping under Allied naval control. Also called **OCA.** (Approved for incorporation into JP 1-02 with JP 3-15 as the source JP.)

ordnance. Explosives, chemicals, pyrotechnics, and similar stores, e.g., bombs, guns and ammunition, flares, smoke, or napalm. (Approved for incorporation into JP 1-02 with JP 3-15 as the source JP.)

oscillating mine. A mine, hydrostatically controlled, which maintains a pre-set depth below the surface of the water independently of the rise and fall of the tide. (Approved for incorporation into JP 1-02 with JP 3-15 as the source JP.)

passive mine. 1. A mine whose anticountermining device has been operated preventing the firing mechanism from being actuated. 2. A mine which does not emit a signal to detect the presence of a target. (Approved for incorporation into JP 1-02.)

percentage clearance. None. (Approved for removal from JP 1-02.)

phony minefield. An area free of live mines used to simulate a minefield, or section of a minefield, with the object of deceiving the enemy. (JP 1-02. SOURCE: 3-15)

pressure mine. 1. In land mine warfare, a mine whose fuse responds to the direct pressure of a target. 2. In naval mine warfare, a mine whose circuit responds to the hydrodynamic pressure field of a target. (JP 1-02. SOURCE: JP 3-15)

pressure mine circuit. None. (Approved for removal from JP 1-02.)

proactive mine countermeasures. None. (Approved for removal from JP 1-02.)

proof. To verify that a breached lane is free of live mines by passing a mine roller or other mine-resistant vehicle through as the lead vehicle. (Approved for replacement of "proofing" and its definition in JP 1-02.)

propelled mine. None. (Approved for removal from JP 1-02.)

protective minefield. 1. In land mine warfare, a minefield employed to assist a unit in its local, close-in protection. 2. In naval mine warfare, a minefield emplaced in friendly territorial waters to protect ports, harbors, anchorages, coasts, and coastal routes. (Approved for incorporation into JP 1-02.)

Q-route. A system of preplanned shipping lanes in mined or potentially mined waters used to minimize the area the mine countermeasures commander has to keep clear of mines in order to provide safe passage for friendly shipping. (JP 1-02. SOURCE: JP 3-15)

reduction. The creation of lanes through a minefield or obstacle to allow passage of the attacking ground force. (JP 1-02. SOURCE: JP 3-15)

reinforcing obstacles. Those obstacles specifically constructed, emplaced, or detonated through military effort and designed to strengthen existing terrain to disrupt, fix, turn, or block enemy movement. (JP 1-02. SOURCE: JP 3-15)

reserved obstacles. Those demolition obstacles that are deemed critical to the plan for which the authority to detonate is reserved by the designating commander. (JP 1-02. SOURCE: JP 3-15)

rising mine. In naval mine warfare, a mine having positive buoyancy which is released from a sinker by a ship influence or by a timing device. (Approved for incorporation into JP 1-02.)

scatterable mine. None. (Approved for removal from JP 1-02.)

ship counter. None. (Approved for removal from JP 1-02.)

sinker. None. (Approved for removal from JP 1-02.)

spoiling attack. None. (Approved for removal from JP 1-02.)

standard pattern. None. (Approved for removal from JP 1-02.)

sterilizer. In mine warfare, a device included in mines to render the mine permanently inoperative on expiration of a pre-determined time after laying. (Approved for incorporation into JP 1-02 with JP 3-15 as the source JP.)

strategic mining. None. (Approved for removal from JP 1-02.)

tactical minefield. A minefield that is employed to directly attack enemy maneuver as part of a formation obstacle plan and is laid to delay, channel, or break up an enemy advance, giving the defending element a positional advantage over the attacker. (Approved for incorporation into JP 1-02 with JP 3-15 as the source JP.)

tactical obstacles. Those obstacles employed to disrupt enemy formations, to turn them into a desired area, to fix them in position under direct and indirect fires, and to block enemy penetrations. (JP 1-02. SOURCE: JP 3-15)

terrain intelligence. Intelligence on the military significance of natural and man-made characteristics of an area. (Approved for incorporation into JP 1-02.)

unexploded explosive ordnance. Explosive ordnance which has been primed, fused, armed or otherwise prepared for action, and which has been fired, dropped, launched, projected, or placed in such a manner as to constitute a hazard to operations, installations, personnel, or material and remains unexploded either by malfunction or design or for any other cause. Also called **UXO.** (JP 1-02. SOURCE: JP 3-15)

Intentionally Blank

JOINT DOCTRINE PUBLICATIONS HIERARCHY

```
                        ┌─────────────┐
                        │    JP 1     │
                        │   JOINT     │
                        │  DOCTRINE   │
                        └──────┬──────┘
    ┌──────────┬──────────┬────┴─────┬──────────┬──────────┐
┌───────┐ ┌─────────┐ ┌─────────┐ ┌────────┐ ┌────────┐ ┌──────────────┐
│ JP 1-0│ │ JP 2-0  │ │ JP 3-0  │ │ JP 4-0 │ │ JP 5-0 │ │   JP 6-0     │
│PERSON-│ │INTELLI- │ │OPERATIONS│ │LOGISTICS│ │ PLANS  │ │COMMUNICATIONS│
│ NEL   │ │ GENCE   │ │         │ │        │ │        │ │   SYSTEMS    │
└───────┘ └─────────┘ └─────────┘ └────────┘ └────────┘ └──────────────┘
```

All joint publications are organized into a comprehensive hierarchy as shown in the chart above. **Joint Publication (JP) 3-15** is in the **Operations** series of joint doctrine publications. The diagram below illustrates an overview of the development process:

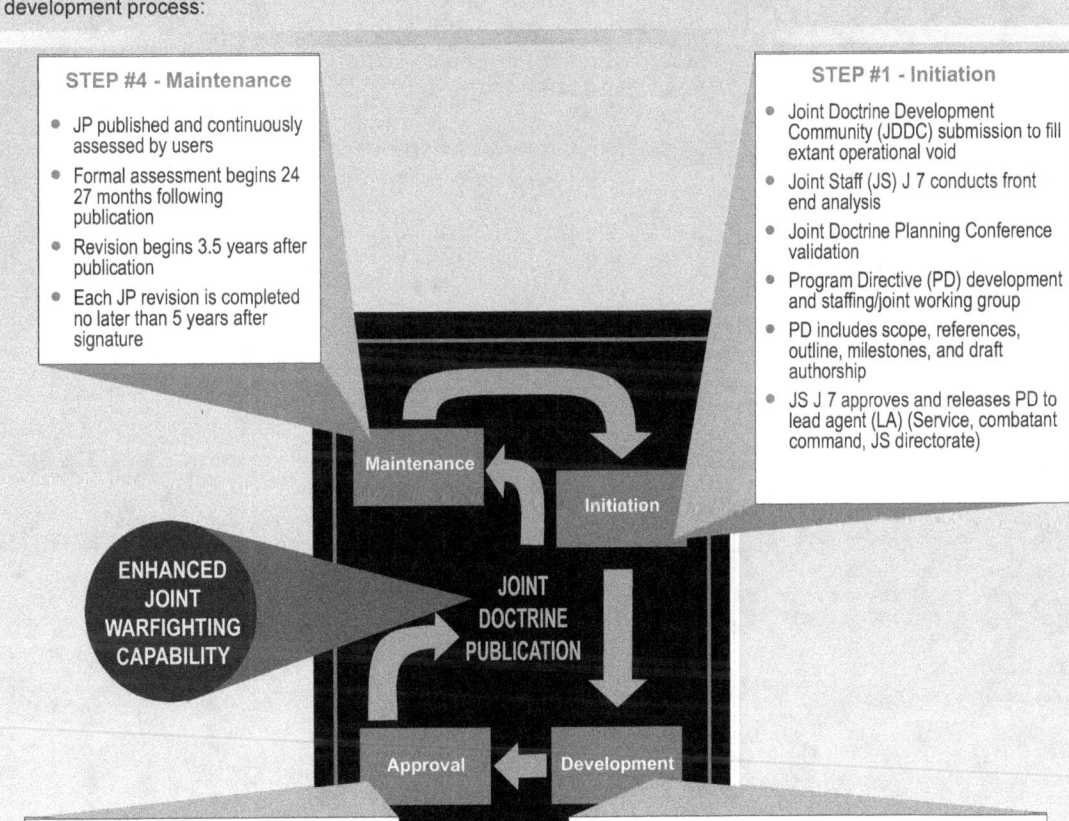

STEP #4 - Maintenance

- JP published and continuously assessed by users
- Formal assessment begins 24 27 months following publication
- Revision begins 3.5 years after publication
- Each JP revision is completed no later than 5 years after signature

STEP #1 - Initiation

- Joint Doctrine Development Community (JDDC) submission to fill extant operational void
- Joint Staff (JS) J 7 conducts front end analysis
- Joint Doctrine Planning Conference validation
- Program Directive (PD) development and staffing/joint working group
- PD includes scope, references, outline, milestones, and draft authorship
- JS J 7 approves and releases PD to lead agent (LA) (Service, combatant command, JS directorate)

STEP #3 - Approval

- JSDS delivers adjudicated matrix to JS J 7
- JS J 7 prepares publication for signature JSDS prepares JS staffing package
- JSDS staffs the publication via JSAP for signature

STEP #2 - Development

- LA selects Primary Review Authority (PRA) to develop the first draft (FD)
- PRA/JS J 7 develops FD for staffing with JDDC
- FD comment matrix adjudication
- JS J 7 produces the final coordination (FC) draft, staffs to JDDC and JS via Joint Staff Action Processing
- Joint Staff doctrine sponsor (JSDS) adjudicates FC comment matrix
- FC Joint working group